Two Oats Club.   1983.

Med många Tul hälsningar från oss alla!

Paul Mentor

Rowyn
Barbara
Sue
David.
Gordon
Carole
Lynette
Annette
Ron. Opie.

The Australian Women's Weekly

Balcony Gardens

The Australian Women's Weekly
Balcony Gardens

Margaret Davis

Golden Press
Sydney

Photography by the *Australian Women's Weekly* on the following pages: 11 (right), 14, 21, 27, 50, 61, 62.
All other photographs, except where acknowledged in the captions, are by the author and her husband, Arthur Davis.

First published 1981 by
Golden Press Pty. Ltd.,
2-12 Tennyson Road,
Gladesville 2111, Australia,
in association with
The Australian Women's Weekly

Printed In Singapore
by Toppan Printing Company

Contents

To the wonderful husband whose constant
help and encouragement made all my
gardening and writing possible.

Preface

I have been a balcony gardener for over six years, having most reluctantly given up a large and much loved garden which my husband and I had created and tended over a period of thirty-one years, and also a smaller, but equally beloved, mountain garden where we grew all the marvellous cold-climate plants and trees.

There must be many ageing couples like ourselves; dedicated gardeners who looked back with sinking hearts to the scenes of former horticultural triumphs and defeats feeling that an enchanting and never-to-be-repeated chapter of our lives had closed forever. And yet, how wrong we were! Our balcony garden has opened up to us a whole new world of fascination and excitement with even more challenges than we met in our two large areas of land, plus the novelty of learning to live in a quite different climate in a quite different country. The nostalgic backward glances ceased soon after we settled into our new apartment, and in their place came a delicious sense of freedom with the realisation that we could now enjoy growing flowers with none of the time-consuming and back-breaking tasks of eternal pruning of too-exuberant branches, sweeping up fallen leaves, watering, watering, watering, and worst of all, weeding, weeding, weeding!

True, the pests are still with us. How they manage to sniff out our treasures in what we thought was a safe hideaway fifteen floors above the ground will forever remain a mystery, and so again began the search for pesticides lethal to only the pests and not to the person wielding the spray. But challenges are the breath of life to gardeners, and how dull it would all be if everything just grew without any effort whatever on our part. But the battle with the pests is only one of those faced by the balcony gardener. Restriction of space also can mean a very difficult series of decisions and sad renunciation of plants that we would so much like to have grown. There is also the frustration of restrictions imposed by building codes which say 'No' to the enclosing, or even partially enclosing of windy open balconies which would provide needed protection for the delicate plants we all long to grow.

I even encountered a neighbour who stoutly maintained that she was allergic to plant life in any form, most especially perfumed flowers, and as she was allegedly slowly dying from the effects of my stephanotis and frangipani, I had to give in to a plea that these be summarily removed. Just when the buds that I had so longingly watched were opening! Even after this was done, I was assured that even the proximity of the foliage of all plants was untenable to this particular allergy, but fortunately other circumstances eventually caused the allergic one to depart, and now we are able to indulge in all the many fragrances that Hawaii's tropical climate provides in such abundance.

In fact, this ability to enjoy the many fragrances at close quarters is perhaps the greatest joy of balcony gardening. This, of course, applies to every climate, for whilst I have the tropical flowers only, the cold and temperate-climate gardener can have a much greater variety. Think of the wallflowers, the stocks, petunias, the exquisite freesias and all the other spring bulbs, and daphne! The list is long, and limited only by the enterprise and enthusiasm of the gardener; and it includes many vines. Vines to twine around doorways and windows, to give beauty as well as perfume; beautiful vines including the morning glory and the heavenly white moonflower. Both flourish in a wide range of climates.

One of the interesting things about balcony gardening is that however experienced a gardener one may have been, there are so many differences that one becomes a beginner all over again. That is why in the very first year of working in this new environment I began making notes, not only for future reference, but in the hope that what I was slowly learning might be of help to others with similar problems, not only the 'oldies' but to the young couples who are starting literally 'from scratch'.

Although this book has been written primarily to help dwellers in apartments, flats, condominiums and units (or whatever name yours may rejoice in), there are still many balconies in what I have called the 'down-to-earth' category — that is, house and terrace-house balconies with a garden just below, to replenish supplies of plants and to conveniently hide spent ones. Such areas can become places of great beauty and relaxation.

HOW TO DEFINE A TERRACE?

The word 'terrace' must surely be one of the most elastic in the English language, stretching as it does from varying-sized balconies to almost any sized level area of ground, even to the marvellously engineered Oriental rice and tea terraces; then up it comes again to describe a row of joined-together houses, many enjoying a renaissance of popularity in recent years. But even these terraces are concerned with growing things, and many small, jewel-like gardens can be seen at both front and back, and these little houses almost always have the added bonus of balconies!

I believe that most of what I have written here will also be of help to those of you gardening on down-to-earth terraces (if yours should be less than jewel-like) but you can ignore the chapter on the problems of watering, you lucky ones, who can spray and splash water about with a hose, with no worry about giving offence to neighbours living beneath.

Although this book was initially, tentatively titled *Balcony Gardening* I was reminded, on a recent return visit to New York (that ancestral home of the highrise) that balconies there, when they are a little larger than usual, become 'terraces' even though they may be twenty or thirty storeys above the ground, just as in Hawaii the term 'lanai' is applied to any balcony of any size, even though the original definition of a lanai, according to my Hawaiian dictionary is 'a porch, veranda, temporary open-sided roofed structure near a house'.

So let us abandon this futile effort to define a balcony and/or a terrace, and get down to the 'nitty-gritty' of making whatever space we have at our disposal, whether it be down on good old Mother Earth, or many storeys up in the sky, as beautiful as we can, and if I have been able to help in any way toward this end, I will not have toiled over this book in vain.

1
Choosing suitable plants

We all have our favourite flowers and plants and will naturally think first of these when starting a new balcony garden, even if it is to be only a small one. Sometimes the location of the balcony happens to be suitable for the plants we want so much to grow, but when space and choice of aspect are necessarily limited, a certain flexibility could possibly avoid some disappointments, not to mention expense. Most plants are fairly expensive these days, and not all balconies have suitable places for raising seeds.

There must inevitably be a good deal of trial and error in this matter, because, even when the aspect seems right, factors such as pollution from car fumes could present problems, and even when this does not arise one sometimes encounters a baffling refusal to grow even from subjects that are generally regarded as extremely hardy. Geraniums can be a classic example of this. They have been so long regarded as the perfect balcony plant, resistant to the greatest neglect and conditions that possibly no other plant would tolerate, yet I have seen ardent geranium lovers almost in tears at their inability to achieve even reasonable results despite the greatest care when these plants are just not in their correct element.

Sometimes moving temperamental plants just a little distance away from one location to another will spark a response. If you do suspect pollution from car fumes is the problem spray your plants at least every day, and more if you can, provided the sun is not shining on them at the time. This spraying, dealt with more fully in chapter 5 (page 12), is extremely important in any case, in order to keep leaves free of the dust which is inevitable in even moderately crowded urban or suburban areas. Plants breathe through their leaves and many also take in nourishment from such spraying, quite apart from the fact that they obviously look a lot better when they are clean.

It is a good idea to look carefully at gardens or potted plants in your area, noting which varieties seem to grow well. This could serve as a rough guide to plants likely to succeed. Every district has its own micro-climate and you must choose plants to suit. In the world of plants there are so many just waiting to be tried that you shouldn't be discouraged if some favourites won't grow in your area. There are, of course, also many plants that will thrive in just about any conditions: the hardy philodendrons, *Ficus* species and all the foliage plants so much used for indoor plantings. These can form a very good background in the shaded areas, and will fill in very well when flowers are scarce.

When choosing flowering plants, try to

1

concentrate on those with a long flowering period, such as the bougainvilleas, in preference to those flowering only in spring. Kurume azaleas for instance are not really good value for balcony use because their flowering period is short, and their foliage not sufficiently attractive to justify a year-round position when space is limited. Some of the Belgian double varieties, on the other hand, will give many months of bloom if the location is ideal. In the case of spring-flowering bulbs, however, this short blooming period would not matter, because they can be dried and stored after flowering, and, of course, annuals are simply discarded after flowering. For those fortunate enough to have a nearby relative or friend with a garden, life becomes a great deal simpler, because plants which are not especially attractive after flowering can be heeled into the soil until the next year, and even items in pots could benefit from an occasional change of scene and possibly additional sunshine.

I have a friend with a large orchid collection who rents a space in a nursery into which his out-of-flower orchids are installed until the time comes for them to bloom

Dendrobium orchids revel in the sun. They will need glasshouse treatment in colder climates, but can be grown outdoors in semi-tropical areas.

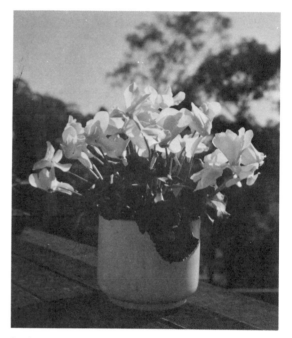

Cyclamen will grow well on a sheltered balcony if given several hours of morning sun.

again. The deal presumably also includes care and feeding during this time. There are, of course, nurseries which will keep up fortnightly supplies of orchids or other plants, and this arrangement could be useful for people too busy to tend the plants, but it would be far too impersonal for those who enjoy caring for their very own plants, and who become attached to them.

So if you are in this latter category (I think that you would not have bought this book if you were not) and if you have found that there is one type of flowering plant which appears to be happy in a particular part of your balcony, consider having a massed display, or a small grouping, of this variety, possibly in different colours, rather than the somewhat 'spotty' effect of a number of different plants mingled together. If possible use the same type and colour of containers. If geraniums are happy with you, then think in terms of a corner stand, or a set of shelves filled with only geraniums. All red gives a wonderful impact. Or if roses are your long suit, then have all roses, even if space may dictate only the smaller types. What could be lovelier than a collection of uniformly potted adorable little fairy roses? For the fortunate ones with the right conditions for gloxinias, the marvellous colours of these gorgeous beauties are wonderful in a mass, and the same protected hour-or-so-morning-sun position would then be ideal for the marvellous long-flowering cyclamen to carry on during the winter whilst the gloxinia bulbs are resting.

I know a lady who found that the tricky but lovely little African violets grew beautifully in her glass-enclosed balcony. She very sensibly concentrated on these, procuring a special stand to go near the window and another trolley-type mobile stand with special lighting on which these beautiful little plants are grouped closely in an absolutely dazzling array. They flower most of the year under these ideal conditions.

This individual grouping also applies to a collection of bonsai, which look far better kept to themselves than when interspersed with other plants. Whatever your climate, there will be bonsai that you can grow. See chapter 17 on this.

In my case, having learned that bougainvilleas and dendrobiums were the plants to be grown here, it soon became apparent that by far the best effect to be had from the former was to keep them by themselves at the warm end of the west-aspected balcony and so I found that by putting them into quite small pots I could fit quite a number on a little cart. I am able to keep up a succession of colour there by relegating those not flowering to another place, and replacing them from my 'reserve' corner. Fortunately, the dendrobium orchids decided that they liked the corner of the living room, where windows on either side and the door to the balcony gave them plenty of light and a good deal of both morning and afternoon sun. It soon became apparent that the corner stand looked far better filled with only these orchids than with a mixture of these and calladiums, and so the calladiums were placed all together on the floor in front to create their own massed effect.

It could take quite a few months of experimentation to ascertain just which subjects prefer just which locations, for these 'micro-climates' can exist even in the small space of one small balcony, but, as Don Watson puts it in his delightful book *Plants are for People,* 'It's bigger than you, this micro-climate, don't fight it, use it and enjoy it!'

These beautiful African violets are growing in perfect conditions beneath the sliding glass windows of an enclosed balcony.

Containers

Providing the best possible containers for growing plants is every bit as important to their appearance as is the selection of a suitable vase for a flower arrangement. After all, your plants can certainly be expected to last a great deal longer than any flower arrangement!

Plants grown as bonsai provide the best possible illustration of the importance of harmony between plant and container. Take any one of those beautifully proportioned little trees growing in its shallow round or rectangular bowl and put it into a dreary black plastic, or even an ordinary red clay pot, and most of its beauty is lost. Unfortunately, most of those glazed Chinese and Japanese pots and bowls which do so much for bonsai are far from cheap, although their beauty and durability make them well worth the additional outlay. There are now many very attractive and less costly plastic and locally made pottery containers to be had. I have even seen a plastic reproduction of the traditional shallow dark brown rectangular bowl so often used for high-grade Japanese bonsai, and, until one picked it up and realised how light it was, it was impossible to detect the difference.

In addition to the pots meant for direct planting (drainage holes are provided) there are many good 'planters' into which growing plants can be set in their existing pots, thereby dispensing with the need for a water-catching saucer. One very good type has a small sunken area at its base, with a sort of small framework on which the pot rests, so that water draining into the base of the planter is kept below the base of the pot. Provided that the water level is watched so that it does not come up to the level of the plant's roots, these planters can provide very valuable humidity in hot weather. The same effect can be produced, of course, by putting a layer of small pebbles or gravel in the bottom of the planter, and this too overcomes the danger of having the plants standing for long periods in water.

You will probably find that very often, especially if this desirable layer of pebbles is provided, the black plastic pots in which most plants are sold will show an ugly too-high rim above your planter. This is not an insuperable problem, especially as most nursery grown plants are set quite low in these pots, and there is quite often a 5- to 8-cm space between the top of the pot and the top of the soil. It is easy to cut away most of this surplus using a sharp kitchen knife. Tie a piece of string or wire around the edge to be cut, so that it will be even. If the plastic is hard, warm the knife in boiling water first. Do not cut right down to the soil level, as you will naturally need to leave a space for retention of water, but this space need not be too deep if you put a layer of sphagnum moss on the soil surface as recommended in chapter 5 on watering. About 1-2 cm of pot rim above the top of the sphagnum moss should prevent overflow of water and give enough grip for lifting the pot out of its planter.

To hold the larger sized pots, plastic

bucket-shaped wastepaper baskets in plain colours can be quite effective. There is a type somewhat narrower than the conventional bucket, but similar in shape. These can be either used for direct planting by simply cutting a hole in the bottom with your kitchen knife, or as holders (or planters) to contain pots. As they are quite deep, it will not be necessary to cut down the sides of the pots that they are to hold; they may even be too deep, but this can be overcome by raising your pot on an inverted saucer or a shallow margarine container, which will fill up the unnecessary depth and serve the same purpose of the layer of pebbles already mentioned: to keep the plant's roots from standing in surplus water.

A search of the supermarkets and gift shops will reveal some quite attractive wastepaper baskets which could serve in this way. You can even use the cheap rectangular deep ones in places against the wall where space is limited and a roomy container is needed for jasmine to be grown flat against the wall. Cut a hole in the bottom and plant the jasmine direct into the wastepaper baskets. Saucers to go underneath can be a problem as round ones won't fit, but painted metal rectangular cake tins will make unobtrusive saucers which take up a minimum of space. If the wastepaper basket you choose is metal, it is not too difficult to cut the necessary drainage hole with an old-fashioned can-opener. Metal and plastic can be painted to match your colour scheme.

There are many types of trough to be found these days and, if these are weatherproof, they can be very useful for holding several pots. They are not usually very deep, so if the pot rims still rise too high, cut them down as much as you can. Instead of putting pebbles or saucers beneath them, get some pieces of absorbent plastic foam and tuck them between the pots (down out of sight, of course). This material is very absorbent. I find it very useful, not only to blot up surplus water in my own two metal-lined wrought-iron troughs, but also at the base of a large hibachi, in which is planted a large plumeria. The incurving edge of this hibachi makes it impossible to see whether there is surplus water under the pot, but with several fairly big pieces of this foam around the sides and base of the pot, I know that surplus water will be satisfactorily absorbed. If you are unable to get this foam, see chapter 5 on watering and drainage for information on using kitchen sponges. The many forms of this plastic foam can be used in a number of ways to help your plants. Incorporate some of the cut-up type sold to fill cushions with the soil in hanging baskets; it will provide useful moisture retention in areas that are not always easy to water. Also the thin sheets can be cut into small circles and put in saucers under pots to serve the same purpose and to absorb surplus water. I also use these sheets, which can be bought in an attractive shade of green, to line the shelves of a small iron plant cart, on which are kept small plants and bonsai. The saucers beneath these are rather shallow, and water can easily spill over the edges unnoticed. With this lining of foam, I know that if this happens I am not likely to be guilty of subjecting my neighbour downstairs to dripping water.

PLANTS IN CANS

One of the balcony gardener's most troublesome tasks is coping with plants sold in those half-rusted cans to which nurseries still cling despite the growing popularity of plastic pots. Unfortunately, the plants that are often the most attractive are frequently grown this way, leaving one no choice but to wrestle with the problem of getting the thing open on arrival home. Sometimes it is possible to find a helpful salesman who will cut down the sides of the can, but if you do not have your new pot ready, or if the soil is very loose, the plant could suffer in the meantime. However, if it is not a very delicate one, and the salesman will cut down the can, wrap the whole thing in a piece of plastic, or a plastic bag to prevent too much soil escaping.

Failing this, possibly the best method of removing the plant from the can is to start at the bottom edge of the can where there are usually two or three holes; insert an ordinary old-fashioned can-opener into each hole and cut upwards. In this way, the rim will not present so much of a problem as trying to cut from the top. Of course, if you happen to have a stout pair of tin snips, they will cope without any trouble, but few apartment dwellers are equipped with a full kit of tools!

Do not try to get the plant out with only one cut down the side of the can; you will almost certainly damage its roots. For small to medium-sized plants, two cuts will usually suffice, but three will be better for the larger sizes, allowing you to lift the plant out with its roots undisturbed. This is very important in the case of such tender-rooted plants as daphne, hibiscus or bougainvillea. Where larger trees are bought in straight-sided round drums, they can often be extracted by allowing the soil to dry, then running a long knife around the edges to loosen clinging roots. Trickle water around the edges only, leave the plant for an hour. Then give more water and leave it to soak in for a short time. Lay the plant on its side. Tap the drum all around and gently pull the plant out. You may need one person to pull whilst another holds the drum. Needless to add, the plant should be well watered once it has been put into its new pot.

This procedure could be followed when re-potting a root-bound plant into a large container. But if it is small enough to invert, it is best to try this first. Spread your fingers across the top of the pot on either side of the main stem, then tip it upside down and tap the edge against the edge of a table or shelf. The ball should then tip out, especially if it is on the dry side or only slightly damp. With a second person to help, this can often be done with fairly large plants if they are not too tall, or alternatively, they can be laid on their sides and the tapping done lightly all around the sides. In the case of breakable containers have some kind of padding beneath. The roots of many plants tend to cling to the sides of cement pots. To avoid this happening in the case of a quickly growing plant that you know will need re-potting again, it is quite a good idea to line the sides of the container with a sheet of plastic, thus ensuring that it will slip out quite easily. Take care that the plastic does not block the drainage hole.

Do not be concerned about the roots that you may sever around the edges of root-bound plants when running the long knife around to loosen them. This is unlikely to cause much injury. It is desirable to loosen and more or less 'tease out' such roots, especially those at the base of the plant in order to prevent them going round and round into a tight ball which will eventually become self-strangling.

Try also to shake out as much as can be safely removed of the old soil, and use only the best quality you can get for replacement. The new soil should be quite dry when you are working it down into the roots. It will then penetrate between them much better than if it is at all damp. Tap the pot up and down to make sure that there are no air spaces, and only then give the plant a good soaking. Don't just water the top, but stand the pot in a saucer of water deep enough to allow the whole soil area to become moist.

The University of Hawaii College of Tropical Agriculture has discovered that poinsettia cuttings planted in white or light-coloured plastic pots develop weak roots as opposed to the strong roots of those cuttings in dark green or black plastic pots. If this is true of poinsettias, it could possibly apply to other cuttings and plants. Therefore it could be that the clear plastic pots now on the market may not provide the dark conditions which roots need to develop. This is certainly worth considering when choosing pots.

Wind poses problems

Wind is almost always the balcony gardener's greatest problem, and it is unfortunately one of the most difficult to solve, especially in the light of the many restrictions placed by councils and often by apartment and unit committees on the enclosing or even partial enclosing of too-exposed balconies. Such restrictions are understandably necessary in cases where balconies are likely to be converted into extra bedrooms which could overload the allowable floor space in large buildings, but it means that we, and our plants, often have to be deprived of what could be a useful and decorative protected garden area.

Sometimes a partial solution can be found by backing too-open railings with sheets of heavy clear Plexiglass secured by a light frame, or using a lighter weight of Plexiglass woven in and out of straight upright railings. Being almost completely invisible, this will offend nobody and will certainly give wonderful protection and added warmth to lower-growing plants.

A decorative iron gate or a not-too-high screen door or trellis secured to the balcony railing at the most windy end would break much of the force of the wind and can also provide a framework to support potted vines or espaliered plants. Take care when wiring such screens to your railings that you don't use a metal which might have a corrosive effect on the existing metal railings. For instance, if the railings are of aluminium which is not anodised they should not be in contact with copper or galvanised wire. If they are anodised, no harm will result, but it would be wise in any case to use covered tie wire to avoid scratching. See chapter 13 on camellias for suggestions for an espalier to train on this type of screen, or against the lower railings if they are not enclosed.

It is possible to sometimes find decorative garden arches of either wire or wood trellis, which, if not too wide, can be placed at one end or in the front of a balcony. The space between the two sides of the arch can be filled with a backing of either similar trellis or a large sheet of Plexiglass, so that vines can be trained over the arch, with the open front then providing a shelter for hanging or tall standing plants. This enables me to grow quite a number of cattleya orchids which thus received protection from too much sun and wind, but many types of hanging plants could take the place of the orchids in cooler areas. Such a situation would be wonderful for baskets of the lovely annual *Schizanthus* (sometimes known as 'poor man's orchid') which comes in such a beautiful variety of colours, but petunias, geraniums and many others would be equally attractive. The baskets can hang not only from the centre of the arch but also from the stays at the sides. They can be secured there by either wire rings which hook on or by handy metal clips made to be clamped to the rims of pots.

I once saw a balcony completely enclosed with wide-meshed chicken wire. This had originally been put there to prevent small children from falling over, but after the children outgrew this danger the wire remained as a support for two decorative but not-too-leafy vines which served to break the force of the wind and to screen out an unattractive view. This leafy screen gave a delightful effect, not only to the balcony area itself, but also when viewed from the rooms beyond. Careful trimming was done from time to time so that the vines did not shut out too much light from these rooms. The type of vine to be used in such cases would depend on the climate, but there are many both annual and perennial suitable for every area. (See chapter 15 on climbing plants for suggestions.)

Where it is not practical to attempt any enclosures, consider having decorative but sturdy trees and shrubs. Many of the evergreens such as the pine family and the so-called pines including the Norfolk Island pine, will stand quite an amount of wind. This Norfolk Island pine from the windswept island for which it was named can be found in a wide range of climates. It looks attractive the year round, and of course, is so useful at Christmas time! When everyone else is scrambling to secure a good-looking cut tree, all you have to do is to lift yours in from the balcony and go to work with the tinsel and baubles which sit so well on its beautifully spaced branches. When these trees grow tall, care must be taken that they are not blown over in very windy weather. This of course, applies to all tall trees. It is wise to pot such trees in cement or heavy pottery containers, and to crock the drainage hole

If strong winds are a problem and you are unable to even partially enclose your balcony, choose wind-resistant plants. These strelitzias will stand up to even the strongest winds. They have attractive bird-of-paradise flowers, but make decorative potted plants even when not in flower.

with some pieces of cement to give added weight. Then put some heavy stones on the soil surface around the trunk. This will give solidity and help to conserve moisture. Look for decorative stones in nurseries or garden suppliers. These can be either the round water-worn ones or the rough, weathered kind from mountain regions. These stones not only have the advantage of giving weight to the pots but also will prevent root damage that could result from the trunks being blown about and loosening roots not otherwise held down. Tying the trunks to balcony railings with covered wire will also help to hold them steady. In cases where there is a cement or brick wall instead of a railing the stone-weighting method is best. If trunks are tied, always be sure to put a small piece of plastic or foam rubber against the trunks to prevent damage by rubbing. See suggestions on other wind-resistant trees in chapter 8.

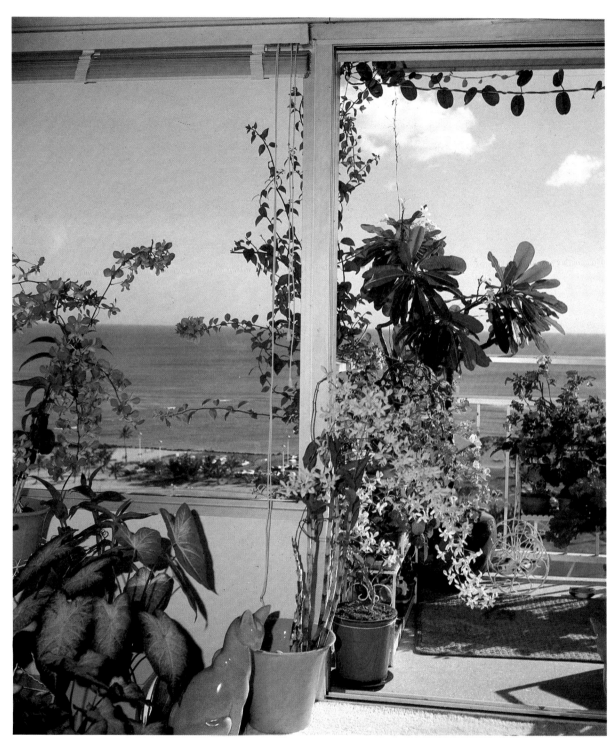

This photograph, showing one end of my living room
with a view of my balcony, emphasises the point that
indoor plants and those on an adjoining balcony can
complement one another.

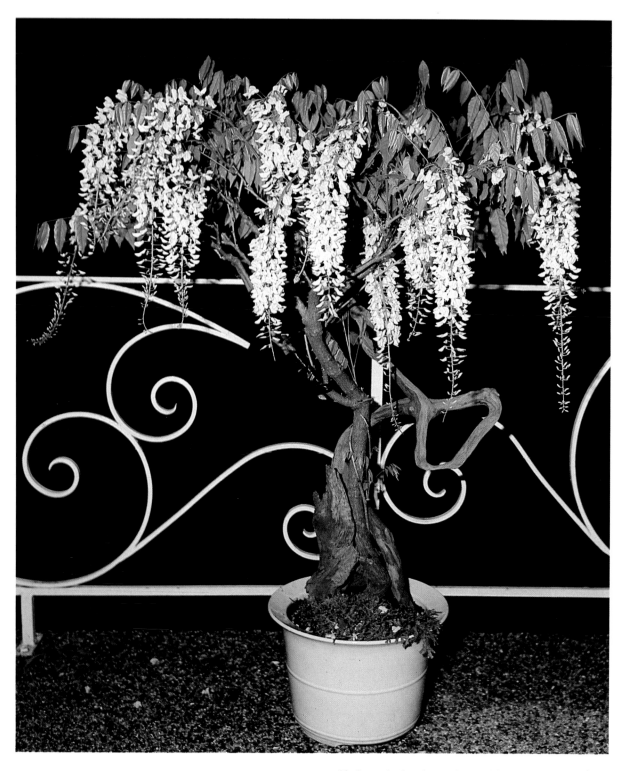

My bonsai wisteria surely provides a convincing argument for installing a light on your balcony! The effect of this, or any plant, is enhanced by the front lighting against the background of darkness. A good deal of patience is needed to grow wisteria in this way, as one will sometimes have to wait for several years for flowering to commence. The final result is worth waiting for. These robust plants must be root pruned twice a year, shortening branches at the same time. They need ample water.

Using your wall space

Even the smallest balcony can usually be counted upon to have a reasonable amount of unoccupied wall area. This can be invaluable for accommodating a wide variety of plants, especially the trailing types which can otherwise be difficult to place. Very often plants on walls will be more protected from the winds which can make life difficult for apartment dwellers *and* their gardens. Quite a number of the more delicate orchids and ferns which I could not otherwise have grown have flourished in these more sheltered conditions. Providing the means of support is, of course, the biggest problem. It will be necessary to obtain or borrow an electric drill to make large enough holes for strong plugs into which hooks can be screwed or, better still, screws long enough to attach a length of trellis to the entire wall. This trellis then enables one to hang any number of pots yet it requires only a couple of strong screws to support quite a large section.

If you are not able to buy the trellis already painted, it will look best painted white. Sometimes trellis is made of rather rough redwood slats, which looks fine on a brick wall, but for white walls it is best to search for the painted kind. In fact, you may have to settle for dismantled garden arches. Some of these arches are in three sections which are intended to be screwed together. Assuming the top section is straight and not curved, you can use all three sections flat on the wall. When we ran out of wall space, I found a narrower arch with sides rather like small ladders and put that up on one of the more protected balcony corners, thus providing a little space for cattleya orchids which needed to hang clear of the wall.

A very useful type of trellis is the concertina type which can be opened and spread to whatever width is required. These provide a wonderful amount of hanging space and are really very decorative when used either as support for climbing plants or as support for hanging pots. It is usually possible to find several sizes in the ring-type wire holders for pots, and you may be able to get clip-on hangers which clamp to the rims of the pots. In order to catch water, it is best to buy the larger ring-type holders so that they can take a light plastic container for the pot. (Be sure to keep a check on these so that water is not retained too long.)

However, if you are using the clip-on type hangers, it is still possible to catch the troublesome water overflow by encasing the lower half of the pots in those circular food covers (like little shower caps) which can be bought in sets. You can make these quite easily from strong clear polythene by simply cutting circles, then hemming them on the machine and running thin elastic through to gather them up to the required sizes. It is then possible to see when there is too much water in the little bags. In the meantime this surplus water, being clear of the roots, is able to provide useful humidity. It may be necessary, in cold weather, to watch out that too much moisture doesn't collect. I have recently tried out this idea for a few hot summer months, so I cannot vouch for its success in really cold climates.

Also you can buy containers with clip-on saucers to take any overflow. Sometimes it is possible to get long narrow rectangular trays that can be used under a narrow trellis, thus avoiding the need to catch water from every pot. These also are very useful to provide humidity.

Where there is not enough space to take any form of trellis, it could be worth visiting specialists in wrought iron to look for attractive iron brackets, some of which will take several plants. These too are very decorative. I have also seen flat-backed hanging baskets designed for outside walls. These look good placed in groups. Wrought-iron brackets can also be used beautifully for hanging baskets, and there are now good-looking plastic hanging baskets in several sizes with built-in saucers both in white and colours. (I use these quite a lot without the wires to hold standing plants, as the clip-on saucers are such a convenience.) They are certainly a vast improvement on the old wire type, which created such water-overflow problems. They also make it easier to use the now-so-popular macrame hangers.

Plants grown in espalier fashion can look very attractive on either large or small wall areas. The range of suitable varieties is great, restricted only by your particular climate. Many plants usually grown as bushes or shrubs will take very kindly to being grown flat against any support, and many look even better this way. A classic case is that of fuchsias,

This decorative corner stand carrying pink azaleas of various types makes effective use of wall space possible.

which are thus given more of the protection they need. This applies also to camellias and quite a number of colder-climate items. For the hotter regions, bougainvilleas and hibiscus will catch more of the sun they love if flattened in this way, as will jasmine, gardenias and all the colourful tropical foliage plants.

I once saw a marvellous idea on a fairly wide balcony, where a beautiful massed garden effect was created by having a series of long narrow-stepped shelves built up against the wall on a framework of concrete building blocks. It was a little like a narrower version of the gay flower-sellers' stalls that are sometimes seen in Europe or in flower markets. This could be used at one end of a balcony where there is often a blank wall. The steps can hold a wonderful array of different plants to be varied according to the seasons. If you did not wish to take the shelves right to floor level, the lowest shelf could be a foot or more up, with a light timber facing to hide the supporting blocks. If there is a handyman available, it may even be possible to have one or two sections of this facing made to pull out like a drawer, where implements and other items could be stored. The

This picture shows that it is well worth going to the trouble of installing lights if they are not already there. All flowers and foliage are enormously enhanced by electric light. What could be more relaxing than sharing a spring or summer evening with them?

shelves can extend almost to the ceiling, giving room for a beautiful tiered effect. On a much smaller scale, an old stepladder can be painted and used with its steps fully opened, and a series of plants placed on each step.

If you can possibly manage to have a small ceiling floodlight mounted above these stepped shelves, it will prove to be the best possible investment, not only for the great added enjoyment you will have from seeing your plants at night (and of course the colours are much intensified and 'glamorised' under artificial light) but also this light will help in giving extra growth and flowers if it can be left on for a few hours each evening. Daylight can be prolonged on short winter days, especially if the special Gro-lux bulbs are used. But even the regular lighting can still be helpful.

All gardens, even the tiniest balcony ones, shoud be given the benefit of lighting, especially in homes where they can be viewed and enjoyed from the living rooms. Even the most plebeian plants and flowers become beautified and transformed under a spotlight or a floodlight. This can be demonstrated by bringing plants indoors and placing them under reading lamps. There are a number of portable lights, some designed for use for barbeques and special outdoor occasions, which will adapt quite well to being hooked up on a bracket or large hook, or even to standing on the floor and tilted upwards — then you wouldn't have to install special wiring.

This practical stand displaying a special collection of maidenhair ferns shows another way of using wall space effectively.

5

Watering and Drainage

It is impossible to stress too strongly the importance of correct and careful watering of balcony plants, not only from your plants' point of view, but also from that of the neighbours in apartments below who can hardly be expected to react favourably to being subjected to sudden showers or even drips from above!

If your balcony is one of the type that has a concrete or brick parapet, there is a good chance that there will be some kind of gutter or depression at its base for drainage of stormwater, and surplus water from potted plants will naturally drain into this gutter, and you will have no further problems. But for those with open-type balconies with either iron or aluminium railings things become much more difficult, especially as the floor will surely slope slightly outward so that any spilled water will be over the edge before you have time to mop it up. Therefore you have to ensure that there are no spills.

The first and obvious answer to this is the provision of a saucer under every pot. The saucer should be deep enough to take a good deal of overflow. But it is sometimes surprising how easy it is to misjudge the amount of water which will drain away from even an apparently thirsty pot, and only experience will help you to judge this. It will help, however, if you can form the habit of going over the plants twice, giving a small amount of water the first time, then doing the rounds again with a second application if there does not appear to be any overflow in the saucer. This will take more time of course, but not as much as it will take to have to carefully empty overflowing saucers and to mop up the water from the surrounding floor area.

A can with as long a spout as possible is an essential. The sprinkler will usually have to be discarded, as these make it too difficult to direct the water into the small space of a pot. Generally, metal cans seem to be the most satisfactory. Some of the plastic ones have somewhat unsatisfactory pouring spouts.

I have found that my watering has been greatly helped by putting a layer of sphagnum moss (sometimes it is known as 'florists' moss') on top of each of my plants. This keeps the plants more moist and also absorbs water better than plain soil, and transmits it gently to the plants as the soil immediately below the moss will be moist enough to absorb the water readily. I hit upon this device after a heavy and prolonged rainstorm had spattered a great deal of soil out of my pots and made a horrible mess all over the balconies. Now, however heavy the rain, it does not beat directly on the soil and only

Finding attractive saucers for pots can be a problem, but these matching saucers, pots and ornamental stands add charm to this terrace grouping of plants. (Photograph by Sir Kenneth Fung.)

water, not mud, has to be mopped up when surplus water overflows. The overflow can be caught by a series of strips of old towelling or some absorbent material, the end of the strip being put into the saucer. This method obviates the heavy work entailed in lifting very large potted plants and trying to empty their saucers. Obviously such methods only have to be employed after periods of very heavy rain.

Sphagnum moss also serves a useful purpose in indicating whether or not water is needed as it is not always possible to determine this in the case of soils which tend to cake or which are dark in colour. It is not necessary to have a heavy layer of this moss, just enough to cover the soil surface will usually be sufficient. Too much could result in the retention of more moisture than is needed in colder climates. If the moss is at all damp, do not water. Remember too, that the rule of not watering in the late evening during cold weather applies as much to potted plants as to those in the open garden. Early in the afternoon is the best time in winter, even though the sun may still be shining on the plants. Do not, of course, water the leaves or flowers whilst the sun is shining on them, but watering the soil, especially if it has this layer of moss to prevent its caking, will do no harm.

In hot weather, evening watering will be quite in order, and then too, the leaves should be sprayed, especially if one lives in a dusty area. It is essential that the leaves be allowed to breathe, apart from the fact that they look very unattractive if coated with dust. Additionally, the moisture absorbed through the leaves will also help the plants' growth.

It is not always easy to find suitable saucers to put under your pots. Those of cement and clay will often be porous, tending to mar the floor beneath, so generally speaking, plastic is the best. For the very large pots, one can often find small round trays to fill the bill. For rectangular pots, such as are used for bonsai, try using the oblong compressed foam trays that hold supermarket vegetables and meat. These are surprisingly durable and washable. The square ones can be useful also, for either square or round pots and, by the way, these take paint beautifully. I usually paint them black, which stays clean longer than white. Painting does help to strengthen these trays also.

Other food containers can be pressed into service too. I have found that a wide dark green round margarine container is very good for holding medium-sized plastic orchid pots. The water drains down to the tapered base, allowing the pot to sit clear and yet to benefit from the condensation from the small amount of water beneath. The base can also be filled with pebbles to produce the same result. Sometimes plastic lids, if not too shallow can be used. Round margarine containers are useful as saucers under small pots. When inverted they also serve very well to elevate most sizes of pots that may be too shallow for their planters, or for troughs.

There is an added advantage in perching pots in this way—it ensures that their bases won't be standing in water, yet if there is some surplus water in the planter it can provide useful humidity without the danger of the plant suffering from 'wet feet'.

I keep an assortment of shallow plastic containers on hand; some held cheeses, savouries of various kinds, dips, relishes, etc. They can be nested together inside unused planters. Another supermarket treasure is the assorted plastic sponges used for cleaning. These, especially the thick ones, are invaluable for absorbing surplus water, either in troughs or planters. I use smaller pieces of these in the planters containing my orchids (*Dendrobium* sp.) tucked at the sides of the pots and under pots on the high shelves of plant stands where it is difficult to look into the planters to check for surplus water.

Undoubtedly a most important piece of equipment for any balcony gardener is a good atomiser. This will be needed in many ways, whatever your climate. If you can get the type with a long extension, so much the better, for with this you can spray the hanging plants and those mounted high on the walls. If your garden has only a few pots, there is a very useful atomiser, made of plastic with a trigger-type handle, which gives a fine spray. I keep several of these on hand for small spraying jobs, together with another plastic type known as the 'High-rise Plant

Small stands can be used instead of saucers if your balcony has a good drainage system.

Waterer and Feeder'. This treasure has an 45-cm-long plastic tube curved at the top, with its other end in a plastic bottle, which is squeezed to eject a jet of water. It is ideal too for hanging baskets, and high-placed plants, and it is far less costly than the larger type of atomiser. Whichever type you use, however, it is very necessary for balcony gardeners to spray their plants daily, especially if you live in a dusty area. This spraying must, of course, be done while there is no sun on the plants, preferably (except in very cold weather) in the late afternoon.

Fertilising

Perhaps it is in the sphere of feeding our plants that the former 'dirt gardeners' have most to re-learn. No longer for us the odorous, but so-effective cow and horse manures! No more of the smelly blood and bone or dried blood. Even the wonderful fish emulsion (although its devotees swear that the smell is short-lived) could perhaps be best left to the great outdoors. True, there are still some packaged forms of poultry humus which are odourless, but these are usually so pulverised as to be light enough to blow away. They can, of course, be mixed with the top layer of soil to help in some way, but generally speaking these manures should be kept on the surface and not brought into contact with plant roots in the confined space of small pots.

Modern science however has come to the rescue with a number of alternatives, perhaps best among them being the pelleted slow-release plant foods. These are not only fool-proof but save a great deal of trouble. They give food for a period of three months. The pellets are scattered on the surface and the nutrients they contain are transported down to the roots when the plants are watered. There are now several combinations to be had in these useful pellets, 14-14-14 being the best all-round type. The numbers refer to the quantities of nitrogen, phosphorous and potash in that order. In 14-14-14 they are present in equal quantities. If your plants already have too much foliage for instance, you need a fertiliser with less nitrogen, so ask for one with a lower first number. These fertilisers are quite odourless and very effective. As with all food for plants in pots, do not overdo.

These slow-release plant foods are usually packaged for use with potted plants, so the directions on the containers will be safe to follow. In the case of the larger packs such as would normally be used in open gardens, quantities given should be halved for potted plants. However, it will usually be necessary to feed potted plants more often, because the nutrients will tend to leach out with the more frequent watering. 'Little and often' is a fairly safe rule, but not *too* often. Remember that more plants die from overwatering and overfeeding than from neglect.

When to feed is another often forgotten consideration. It is quite important to realise that plants, like people, need a rest period, and this is usually (unlike people) taken in winter. It is therefore not at all good to try to force a resting plant into untimely growth at this time. Deciduous plants show quite clearly when they are resting by simply dropping their leaves, but the evergreen types do not give such clear signals. A slowing of growth at summer's end should also mean a slowing of food application. When the plants are dormant, it is best to cease feeding altogether till spring growth begins. Then you can be generous, and continue to be whilst growth is active and the food is needed for the new growth.

Whilst the stimulation of lush foliage

growth by using spray-on foliage fertilisers can be fine for indoor plants, it must be used with discretion on those exposed to wind and sun, lest the leaves become battered and burnt. But if your position is protected, you could try using one of these. They are absorbed through the leaves and can be dramatically effective for both flower and leaf growth. Be sure to observe directions on the container, which will surely contain a warning against spraying whilst the plants are in sun. Late afternoon is usually the best time. It is always desirable to spray again with clear water 24 hours later, to remove surplus residues which could be harmful.

There are still other soluble plant foods especially made for potted plants, some to be given a few drops at a time when watering, and some to put on the soil and then watered in. All are good if used as directed. Remember that the paramount rule for feeding plants whether in the ground or in pots is that the soil should be moist before applying food in powdered, granular or pelleted form.

A special word of warning on feeding should be given to those who are growing citrus trees in pots. As I have said in chapter 14 on citrus, it is a good idea to get special citrus food if possible, but remember that this food is usually packaged with open-ground trees in mind. In some countries instructions are given according to the age of the tree, for example 500 g per year of growth. This kind of application given to a tree in a pot or tub would spell disaster! Citrus trees do appreciate small doses of poultry humus, but

as mentioned earlier the light powdery material is likely to blow away.

You can overcome this by spreading it on the surface and then covering it with a layer of sphagnum moss. This will not only prevent its blowing away but gently speed its absorption into the soil. It is good practice to have this layer on all potted plants, as, when there is heavy rain, the moss will also prevent the spattering of soil on to the floor of the balcony. Even though sphagnum moss is becoming rather expensive, the cost is really worth it as the moss helps retain moisture in the soil and saves you quite a deal of watering time.

It is very useful to keep a small notebook in which to enter dates of fertiliser given in cases where only monthly or 3-monthly applications are required, *especially* for the latter, because even good-memory people get a bit hazy after 3 months! In the back of the same little book you can record bits of useful information, records of other people's successful results with particular plants, and even times of flowering of special items can be handy for reference. Much of the material for this book came from such jottings of my own experiences and successes or failures. For larger-scale reference, an index file with clippings of articles by experts on particular plants (but make sure they *are* experts), longer notes on your own experiences and successes worth remembering for next year, stores where various supplies were bought (how often we forget these when we want the same items later!), and even nurseries.

7

Storage of equipment

One of the balcony gardener's problems is finding a place to store not only items such as empty pots and saucers, bags of soil, dormant bulbs, drainage material and, worst of all, insecticides and fertilisers. Fertilisers probably create the biggest problem by reason of the unhelpful habit of many manufacturers of packaging these in nothing smaller than 2.5 kg bags! Often the sizes are even larger, many going up to 10 kg. I would very much like to appeal to these suppliers to give more thought to the ever-increasing army of balcony and other small-scale gardeners who have simply no place to store these large and often smelly packages. Occasionally a search will reveal one of the smaller garden shops where the proprietor will be helpful enough to split up the large bags of superphosphate or 10-30-10 fertiliser into manageable small plastic bags. It could even be worth while proposing that your local garden club suggest this course to nearby dealers. Alternatively, clubs, or possibly groups of neighbours, could get together in doing a little bulk buying and portioning out, thus saving on costs.

Even so, these items are hardly suitable for storing in kitchen or bathroom closets, and the balcony itself is the logical place. Much will depend on available space, but perhaps a small cupboard could be located at one end of the balcony. If it is low enough plants can stand on it when it is not in use as a potting place.

When we bought our apartment it contained several items of furniture which we did not want to keep. One of these was a metal patio table about a metre square, another was a sort of traymobile about a metre long on which the TV set stood. As this was a rather ugly brown affair, it was relegated to the balcony, under the table, which was then placed at one end against the wall. This makes an excellent place for some taller plants at the back, and the table area in front is large enough for re-potting. Materials for this are kept on the traymobile beneath, which is then wheeled out when required and afterwards goes back under the table. It has two shelves and carries pots, bags of fertilisers, charcoal, orchid mix, etc. All this is then completely hidden by a wrought-iron firescreen which just fits across the front of the table and also conceals a pile of larger pots and bags of soil which are too large for the traymobile shelves and stand at the side. I achieved an extension of the firescreen by laying another unwanted metal table on its side, with its top facing outward, and a basket containing tools and more potting material hides behind this.

8
Trees for balconies & terraces

Whatever your climate, there will be quite a range of small trees and large shrubs available for balcony conditions. Naturally the evergreen type will be more widely preferred, but even deciduous trees often have a beauty of form, in some varieties, which endures even without the added attraction of leaves. And what a joy it can be, when spring comes, to watch the rapid unfolding of leaf buds to the marvellous golden-green of newly opened leaves! Every bit as pleasant as watching flowers open from the bud stage.

I am thinking, somewhat nostalgically, as I write this, of the lovely delicate maples, some with leaves like the finest lace. Trees to be treasured, and to be given the most sheltered position you can find, for any wind will spoil them. If given this shelter, or even brought into the house whilst the leaves are young and tender, they will make a beautiful house decoration, and will stand up to indoor conditions for months. They can then be taken out of doors in periods of calm weather. (If the tree is large a wheeled platform is very useful.) Some of the maples are sturdier than the fine-leaved Japanese varieties: the large-leaved sugar maple (*Acer saccharum*), the common European or English field maple (*Acer campestre*) and the box elder (*Acer negundo*) are only a few of the many varieties which grow into very large trees, but will also grow for quite a few years in not-very-large pots if given good soil and plenty of moisture. The sugar maple was one of many that I grew in this way. I used to keep it in the house and on the balcony during the entire summer.

Then there is the lovely golden-leaved *Acer japonicum aureum* with its unfolding leaves looking just like groups of half-opened fans. The leaves of this one are sturdier than most, but will still tend to curl and burn if exposed to heavy wind and strong sun. Of the more than one hundred species of maple, the Japanese, smaller-leaved varieties cover a wide range of colours and forms, all of them wonderful in both spring and autumn. The best known is the common type, *Acer palmatum,* which covers the hillsides of Japan with brilliant reds and golds, sending thousands of tourists in autumn to revel in the marvellous spectacle. But you can have a small-scale spectacle on your own balcony and if you have shaped your small tree attractively, it will blend quite well into the background during the winter months. There are so many lovely variations of this Japanese maple that it is worth searching around the nurseries for them if you have sufficient room for several. Perhaps the most beautiful is *A. dissectum viridium* with delicately lacy serrated leaves, and this comes in a dark red form also. *A. scolopendrifolium* is almost as lovely, with longer, fine, somewhat spidery leaves. Both of these have a very graceful habit of growth. Then there are lovely foliage variations in *A. reticulatum,* with palest green leaves edged and veined in darker green, and a similar form with rosy edging. A number have dark reddish leaves and there is a lovely medium green one with larger leaves and a more upright habit called *A. filicifolium.*

Although one usually sees them in the form of very large trees, the willows can be very easily tamed into growing beautifully in either large or small pots, and are so easy to root from either long or short cuttings. I've had a lot of fun in the past shaping them into bonsai and larger forms, and greatly regret that they, like the maples, will not grow in this tropical region where I now live, because they give such quick and decorative results. In either cool or semi-tropical climates a cutting taken in spring, or even in summer, will root in just a few weeks if kept in a deep container of water (with a little piece of charcoal to keep the water sweet). It can then be potted into rich soil where it will continue to grow rapidly to whatever height you require. If the pot is kept in a deep saucer this will help to retain the wet conditions that these trees prefer. So rapid will growth be if the climate is suitable that the roots may need to be pruned twice a year. This is not difficult with such a hardy specimen as the willow. You pull the tree out of its pot (dry it off for a day or two first, as it can be a very soggy operation on a balcony otherwise) and slice off about a third of the packed roots with a sharp carving knife. I am assuming that the pot will be quite full of

roots and very little soil by this time. If it isn't, it does not yet need to be pruned. Replant it in the richest soil you can get, then give plenty of water and return to the water-filled saucer. It is necessary to prune back some of the top growth at the same time to compensate for the reduced root system. Take off about a third also.

Generally speaking, most of the other deciduous trees have a less graceful habit than the willows and maples, and therefore can look less attractive when bare. This is an important point to be considered where space is limited. Where there is a big area such as in a penthouse garden, one can indulge in such deciduous shrubs as *Weigela,* and in fruit trees which compensate for their bare period with lovely blossoms and fruit. For the limited areas, the best fruit trees are those of the citrus variety. So enamoured am I of all the citrus that I feel I must give them a section to themselves (see chapter 14, page 38), lest this chapter become too long.

Let us turn to the taller trees, and consider some that might be used to hide an ugly view or to give some summer shade. The universally popular *Ficus* genus, with large-leaved *F. elastica, F. decora,* and *F. lyrata* are ideal here, and can be moved indoors in freezing weather, as can that darling of the interior decorators, *Ficus benjamina* (weeping fig).

Ficus spp. are very amenable to shaping. In fact it is a good idea to start with a single-stemmed plant in the case of *F. benjamina* and, unless you have a good deal of space, keep the side growths short, because being a weeping tree it will look its best if grown tall, with the branches then drooping downward. In the case of the choice maples, most of these are grafted on to understock of the common Japanese type, and are therefore already usually in a weeping form, being naturally soft and pendulous. The Japanese common one can be shaped in many ways, see chapter 17 on bonsai.

Another indoor-outdoor favourite,

which is also very hardy, is the Queensland umbrella tree (*Schefflera actinophylla*) which appears in a wide range of climates. This is a naturally tall grower, having strong cane-like stems. It is ideal for places where you need some height.

There are many conifers, and the more compact types could be very useful. Also I have seen *Cedrus deodara* and several forms of spruce (*Picea*) growing well in containers. Then there is the Norfolk Island pine, so useful at Christmas! Keep Norfolk Island pines moist, but not soggy, to prevent drying out of lower branches. Spraying each evening will also help to provide the humidity they need. They are very hardy in most climates, asking only a reasonably good soil and occasional fertilising.

Although not strictly a tree, bamboo, suitable for the warmer climates, is extremely decorative, and I have seen it used in a long trough forming a quite thick screen where the view was not good. It will also give quite good wind protection. Also for the warmer regions, the frangipanis (*Plumeria* spp.) are ideal, especially the evergreen Singapore variety. The deciduous types are not bare for long in tropical climates. I have six of different colours on my balconies, and all are a joy, giving marvellous perfumes all through the summer and standing up to wind better than most trees. Their root system is not very large and they seem to be quite amenable to growing in not-very-large containers. Of course, the heavy top growth, with such thick branches, dictates a reasonably large pot, and there is always the problem of not overpotting newly rooted cuttings as these will rot if given too much soil. Therefore in their early stages give them a deep but not too wide pot, and tie the stem to the railing if possible, or to a stake.

It is possible to start quite big branches as cuttings, but it is important to dry these well before planting. Four weeks is not too long to let them stand in the shade out of doors before putting them into soil.

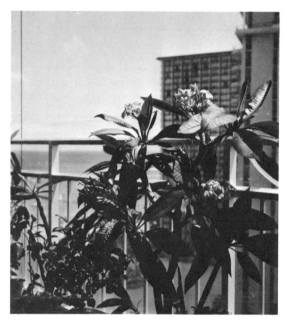

The hardy, fragrant *Plumeria sp.* (frangipani) is a good tree for windy balconies. It can be grown in a reasonably large pot for quite a few years if fed regularly. The flowers continue right through the summer and autumn. A warm sunny position is essential. As well as the common yellow deciduous form there are other deciduous types and an evergreen white Singaporean variety. They all do well in pots or tubs.

If the cutting has been taken whilst in leaf, cut the leaves off, leaving about 1-2 cm of stub which will subsequently drop off. It is extraordinary how these cut branches will continue to produce leaves and flowers without any water for so long. There must be a great deal of food stored in those thick fleshy stems! They must be watered sparingly until well established. Then they can be given a general slow-release fertiliser three or four times a year.

That symbol of the tropics, the coconut palm, is wonderful on balconies for breaking the force of too much sun, or even just for decoration. They are the easiest of palms to grow, being content with ordinary beach sand, or if this is not available any soil will do. They also can get by with a pot just large enough to take the coconut which remains with the sprouting plant, but again there is the problem of supporting the heavy top. My two are tied to the railing, if only to hold them upright when the strong winds blow. It can be a slow business growing your tree from a coconut. It is better to buy a sprouted one from a nursery, or you may know somebody with palms in their garden which are very likely to have sprouted nuts beneath.

There are, of course, many smaller varieties of palm suitable for growing outdoors, but not all are sun-hardy. Again it is a matter of getting the type suited to your own climate. Some will stand reasonably cold conditions but, like *Ficus* and the camellias, would be best brought indoors when temperatures get very low. Some, like the much-used indoor palms, will not even demand a well-lighted position when indoors. For balconies in warmer or temperate areas a coffee tree is well worth trying. It is doubtful whether you will be harvesting your own beans, but it has very pretty flowers and glossy pendulous leaves. A medium-sized tree could even produce a few beans if the location is favourable, but this would have to be quite a hot area. I have seen coffee trees grown as indoor plants quite effectively. They will grow quite tall if given a slightly acid soil which holds water well as they need to be fairly moist and of course must have some sun.

If you are lucky enough to have a fairly large trough, it is possible to grow quite big trees. I was amazed when speaking some years ago with Ralph Hancock, who created the famous Derry and Tom's roof garden in London and the marvellous International Gardens on the Rockefeller Centre roof, to learn that the former garden had less than 45 cm of soil, yet it contained a number of birches, many very large shrubs and a number of other quite big trees. The secret is good feeding, and rich soil to begin with.

If possible, ascertain which of the trees you would like to grow have large root systems. Those such as the willows, as I have explained, have such fast-growing roots that frequent root pruning will be essential, but the camellias, on the other hand have a much slower and less ram-

pant root growth, and will need potting on only every few years even though top growth may be quite large. Rate of growth depends on the variety. Catalogues of good camellia specialists will give information on this, once you decide on the variety you prefer. See chapter 13 on camellias. Frangipanis too, although fast growers, do not have very big roots when grown in pots. A bay tree of any size will prove itself a great treasure. (For more information see chapter 19 on herbs.)

One of the best balcony garden trees I have ever seen was growing on the balcony of a thirtieth floor penthouse. It was a 3.5-m Australian weeping bottlebrush.

The popular weeping fig (*Ficus Benjamina*) grows well on a not-too-windy balcony and can be moved in for indoor decoration, as shown here.

The hardy Norfolk Island pine grows in a great many climates. An ideal balcony tree which can be brought inside to make a very good Christmas tree.

Annuals for colour

Although they are inevitably transient, and require a certain amount of maintenance, nothing can quite equal the gaiety of spring and summer annuals. They can be used in so many ways; they can serve as fill-ins whilst the more permanent vines and trees are growing, and can also be combined most effectively with these at any time.

One beautiful New York balcony garden features annuals in combination with evergreen trees in tubs. Pansies are lovely used in this way; but of course pansies are lovely used in *any* way. What would spring be without these adorable masses of little faces? They are especially lovely when combined with tulips, and although this is so often done in garden beds, it can be just as effective in pots or larger tubs and troughs. The beauty of this arrangement is that the pansies hide the dying tulip foliage very effectively, and then continue on their merry way right through the summer, asking only an occasional application of fertiliser and the removal of dead flowers. But if you do not live in tulip country, there are other bulbs with which this arrangement can be carried out. Pansies can combine with any number of perennial plants and flowers. There is a great variety to be had in size

and shape of pansies, and in the smaller-flowered violas, and all are lovely. They look attractive in hanging baskets too, either alone or combined with other flowers. (See chapter 16.)

The idea of combining several kinds of annuals is well worth considering. I saw some delightful examples of this in Europe recently. There were troughs with tall snapdragons at the back, then a row of medium-height marigolds, then pansies in front. In larger tubs or pots there is a lot of scope, for one can use such tall things as cosmos, lupins, delphiniums or marguerite daisies at the back, medium marigolds, snapdragons, salvia, or zinnias for the next tier, and in front either pansies, petunias, alyssum or lobelia. The wonderful blue of lobelia combines beautifully with so many other colours, especially the bright red of geraniums, and if to these two is added a border of white alyssum or candytuft the effect is really stunning.

Geraniums are almost inseparable from windowboxes, obviously because they are the hardiest of flowers, standing up to a great deal of wind, sun and even neglect, if the climate is right for them. In areas where humidity is high and summers too hot, they can be subject to rust and will often develop a 'leggy' growth, whereas in cooler areas they stay beautifully compact. Where winters are really cold, they are usually treated as annuals, and their abundance and cheapness plus the endearing ease with which they grow from cuttings make it hardly worth while trying to keep plants in the garden all year. If you are a geranium fan, it is well worth while going to the shows staged by the numerous geranium societies to see the new colours and forms which appear each year. There are usually attractive ideas for displaying these old favourites at these shows, many of which are adaptable for balcony and terrace settings.

Probably the closest runner-up to geraniums in popularity would be the equally colourful petunias. Certainly they outdo the former in range of colour and form, and they too are extremely hardy. Their perfume certainly gives them a definite edge, and even a few in a pot can be wonderfully fragrant on warm summer evenings.

There are many new varieties and combinations of colour every season. Like most of the annuals they will continue to flower much longer if spent flowers are regularly removed. The cascade types are very good for planting around the edges of troughs or tubs to spill down, and of course they are ideal for hanging baskets.

There are several ways of acquiring annuals. They can all be raised from seed, either sown direct where they are to grow and thinned out later, or in shallow pots or boxes. Be guided by the directions on each package as requirements vary; some need no soil cover at all, others should be covered either lightly or up to about 7 mm in depth.

If you do not plan to grow enough to make seed-raising worthwhile, you can buy either small seedlings or wait for plants already in flower in small pots. This way, you are certainly able to select your colours, and for only a small number it can be worth the extra cost. Give them really rich soil when they are past the seedling stage. It is far easier to buy ready-mixed packages, as trying to make suitable mixes can be very messy on a balcony. The packaged ones are all sterilised and will contain, in most cases, enough nutrients to last until your plants are well established. The balcony gardener is usually lucky enough to avoid the slugs and snails which plague annuals in the open garden, even though there will still possibly be other pests to contend with.

Use a quick-acting liquid fertiliser when flowering commences, especially after the first flush of bloom when spent flowers and stems are cut back ready for a new crop. This cutting back can take the form of shearing in the case of small compact items such as candytuft. It will also stimulate more side growths. For this reason too, it is good to nip off the tops of the larger subjects in their early stages so as to get more compact bushy growth, even though a top bud may be close up. It must be remembered that, with only a few exceptions, annuals, like vegetables, need a lot of sun, but as sun will inevitably move seasonally, it may be helpful to consider using a wheeled traymobile or a portable stand to chase it up when necessary. Where space permits there are also troughs fitted with casters, or casters can be added to existing troughs.

Where there is really only a little sun, try concentrating on such plants as cinerarias, polyanthus, primulas, balsam, impatiens and fuchsias. Fuchsias do not come in the category of annuals of course, so more details on these are given in chapter 16 on hanging baskets. There are also a number of very colourful bromeliads, some with flower spikes and some with leaves as gay as flowers, which will grow in shaded places.

This also applies to the very attractive coleus, with its great variation of leaf shades. Some of these will require only a little sun. Experience will soon show which seem to need sun, as you will find that they acquire a drawn, leggy look if they are in too much shade.

If you have an aspect with only summer

sun, it could be worth investigating the idea of a shelf attached to the railings which will drop down when no longer needed to give more space in the sunless periods. Hinged in the manner of a drop-sided table, I have seen such shelves used for outdoor dining on not-very-wide balconies where there are timber railings, but they could equally well serve as seasonal plant holders. Such a shelf could also be mounted on any wall, and could serve alternatively as a temporary work bench, being dropped down when more seating space is needed.

Having experienced the frustration of having a balcony end which had full sun one month, and none the next, I would suggest that you consider the lightness of the containers and soil even if wheeled carts or troughs do not fit your setting, so that lifting them from place to place will not ruin your sacroiliac. For that reason, the ready-mixed soils are much easier, as they usually contain a portion of light-weight peatmoss or other water-retaining mediums which also help to keep the soil open. Remember that annuals need to be kept well watered, but if you spray them from overhead, as you should do to keep dust from settling on them, be sure to avoid doing this when the sun is shining on them. Usually late evening is a good time, except at times when there is a danger of nights being very cold.

In India, where a great many annuals are grown in the all-too-brief spring before the searing sun cuts their lives short, I have seen wonderful borders of many different plants all growing in pots, arranged with the tall ones behind and grading down through several heights to low ones in front. One ardent gardener I met had no less than 2,000 such potted plants, all annuals. Realising the transient nature of both the plants *and* the Indian spring, I asked what happened to the pots after the flowering had ceased, and it seems they are stowed away on the roof! Now whilst one must concede that few balconies would allow potted borders on this scale, the idea could perhaps be modified, with pots no longer occupied being stored in a garage or storage area. Plastic ones are recommended for ease of lifting and storing. Also they are vastly cheaper.

When selecting plants to be grown, think about trying the lovely quick annual morning glories in pots with wire supports if you haven't space to let them climb. (See chapter 15 on climbing plants).

If your balcony receives only a little sun try growing a collection of polyanthus. They come in many colours and will make a marvellous display.

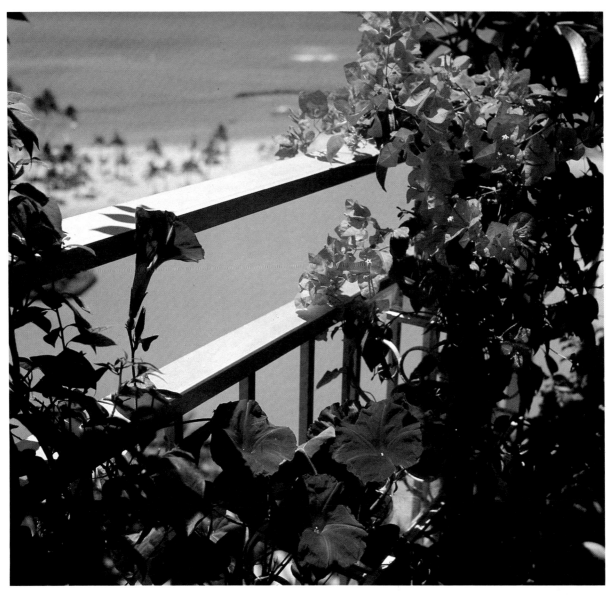

Teamed here with a mauve bougainvillea is one of the hybrid annual ipomoeas. These are wonderful for quick effects in either hot or cold climates. If you find a good variety it is worthwhile saving seeds.

The annual ipomoea, or *Convolvulus* 'Heavenly Blue', grows rapidly and beautifully in both warm and cool climates. It actually lasts much longer in temperate or cool climates, as our tropical heat causes the flowers to wilt very quickly, but I love its colour so much that I grow it each spring around the balcony doors.

The bamboo hedge in the long trough on this terrace provides a wonderful solution where more privacy is needed. The light foliage completely screens from view the adjacent wing of the building besides providing shade from the too-strong tropical sun. The pink flowering plant is Mussaenda, Queen Sirikit, a very attractive tree mainly confined to tropical regions.

One side of the penthouse garden of Mr Stewart Mott contains a variety of vegetables, a trough of herbs, a grapevine, roses and, in the background, several trees.

10

Roses

Undoubtedly the perfect rose for the balcony gardener is the adorable little miniature or 'fairy' rose, not only because of the very small amount of space it requires but also because its blooming period is far longer than that of the larger varieties. It can be grown in any but the most extreme of climates and has actually been known to bloom quite happily under a layer of snow. It seems to have originated in Switzerland, where Dr Roulet, for whom the smallest of the species is named, saw it growing on the windowsills of houses in the small village of Mauborget. The native people of the village assured him that it had been grown there for centuries, always in pots in the houses as it was regarded as being too small and delicate to grow outdoors. The doctor secured some cuttings which were propagated by M. Correvon of Geneva, who named them 'Rosa rouletti'. Since that time a great many other forms and colours have evolved and it is now possible to have a beautiful collection of these enchanting little miniatures in a quite small area.

They show a definite preference for growing in pots: when grown in open ground they tend to lose the compact shape which is their greatest charm. Some types grow to only 5 to 8 cm in height, but others will grow from 15 to 30 or 38 cm, but all have perfectly proportioned tiny flowers and leaves.

Contrary to the belief of the Swiss villagers, these roses are extremely hardy, flower continuously from early spring until late autumn and require a minimum of care. In hot summers it is best to give them shade from midday sun, but generally they prefer a sunny position, although they can get by with partial sun. Opinions vary as to pruning, some growers maintaining that all that is needed is the cutting off of spent flowers, taking the stems to just above the lower shoot, which keeps the plant shapely. Certainly this would probably be all that is needed for the very tiny varieties, but the taller ones could take harder cutting in early winter. Dead wood should be pruned off at all times.

Unfortunately these tiny roses are just as attractive to pests as their larger relatives, especially during hot weather, but it should not be difficult to keep an eye on them and take steps at the first signs. Easily spotted are the aphids, and they can easily be removed with thumb and finger from the buds and new growth where they first appear. (Do not rush for the spray gun unless really necessary.) And if, as I hope, you are spraying with water daily (after the sun has left them) a fine jetting under the leaves should keep red spider mites away. Do not do this spraying too late in the day if weather is cold. Red spider mite is a pesky microscopic insect. It is usually green with black markings and is only red during a short period of its hibernation. It lays its eggs in a fine whitish web, and its presence is indicated by yellowish-grey blotches on the leaves. Cut off any leaves you see with these signs, and spray with soapy water (do not use detergent) and spray again with clear water within 15 minutes. It should not be difficult to check these little plants for pests as the pots are so small and easy to lift up to check under the leaves.

They will probably be in 75-mm or 100-mm pots when you buy them, and this size should be adequate for the smaller types for quite a time. The bigger-growing ones may need to go into 127-mm pots after a year or two, but, as with most plants, it is better not to overpot. For this reason some fertiliser should be given monthly during the growing season, or failing this, give a three-monthly application of the pelleted slow-release plant food which is scattered on the surface of the soil and gradually absorbed as plants are watered. These slow-release fertilisers are good for many plants as they have the advantage of preventing the risk of over-fertilising, especially in the case of tiny plants like these which can be killed by too strong fertiliser. Always water the soil first whichever type you use, and then water it in after applying.

Watering must also be done with care, being sure that the pot is well drained. Especially whilst growing, these plants

This lovely climbing rose ('Nancy Hayward') beautifully ornaments a balcony railing. (Photograph by Stirling Macoboy.)

should not be allowed to dry out. On the other hand they must not be watered if the soil surface is already wet. During their short resting period in winter give less water.

There have been many new introductions to the ranks of these lovely little plants since the original *rouletti* was propagated, and all are beautiful. A choice is hard indeed. There are pinks such as 'Bo Peep', 'Sweet Fairy', 'Cri Cri'; the reds include 'Beauty Secret', 'Zwergkönig', 'Fire Princess' and 'Starina'. There is a lovely white, 'Pixie', several yellows, lavender, salmon, even some with pink and white in their tiny 13-mm-wide flowers. Do try to have at least one in your balcony garden, but I am sure you will want more when confronted with the task of having to choose, and certainly this is one instance when choice is not hampered by the problem of lack of space!

If you do not suffer from lack of space, however, and still hanker after full-sized roses, there is no reason why you cannot grow these in pots. Many varieties take quite well to this. If you can use the climbing types in the background, with other plants in front, the problem of their bare stems in winter will not be so great. One often sees climbing roses in pots in Italy; in one hotel in Portofino, famous for its flowers, large urns of roses are intermingled with ancient wisteria, all romping happily together over pergolas on a large terrace; in another hotel we saw them trained against a lattice screen, and many of the polyantha type are used on balconies all over Europe. Even quite rampant varieties can be tamed to grow as bonsai. I had good results with two old-fashioned favourites, the yellow 'Banksia' (thornless, happily) and pink 'Seneca Anemone'.

Roots may possibily need pruning after a few years if they are planted in very small containers, but in reasonably large pots or urns they will grow for many years provided that fertiliser is given regularly. One must, however, be sure to get the right type of heavy soil for these roses, as the normal packaged all-purpose mixes is too light for the roots which insist on firm anchorage, especially where wind is strong. Go to a rose specialist nursery for your soil if the pot in which the roses are bought is not large enough. If, after several years you feel that your roses need more space or if the roots appear too crowded and you want to plant them back in the same pots, it is no big problem to root prune them. This should be done in late winter. Turn them out of the pots, knock off old soil, and with a sharp knife or cutters, trim off 5 to 8 cm from the sides and bottom roots. Give good quality new soil and water well.

Many specialists sell beautiful standard, or tree, roses in both miniature and full-sized varieties. These are grafted on tall straight stems of varying heights, and look very attractive in containers.

For choice of varieties of roses to grow, it is best to go to a local nursery and be guided by their recommendations, as, like many plants, roses, whilst thriving in most climates, still have preferences to give of their best.

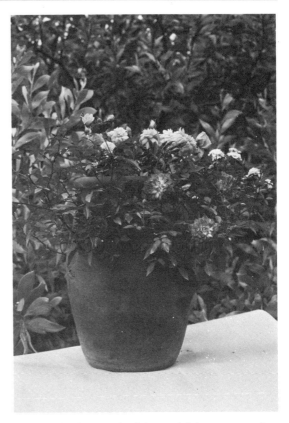

The short bushy growth of these miniature roses makes them an ideal choice for balcony garden pots. This strawberry pot has Gold Coin (top), Jeannie Williams (left), Lori Nan (centre) and Marylin.

11
Bougainvilleas for warm climates

It must surely be safe to say that no flowering plant can surpass the brilliant bougainvillea for use as a potted plant in areas where the climate can supply its need for warmth and hot sun. This need not necessarily be a fully tropical climate; if the right varieties are chosen they can be grown in semitropical and subtropical regions (I grew a few very satisfactory bonsai specimens in cool climates) but they must be given as much sun as possible at all times.

In Hawaii they are in their element, especially on the Big Island of Hawaii's Kona coast, a low-rainfall area with incredibly poor-looking volcanic lava. The roots apparently find something to their liking in this unlikely looking medium as the bougainvilleas romp in a marvellous profusion of bloom and colour. They seem able to get by without actual soil as it is known to the average gardener and even in Honolulu I have bought plants from nurseries potted only in a fine gravelly mixture. Yet those I have grown in an ordinary house-plant mix also do very well, so it does seem as though the growing medium can vary widely so long as good drainage and plenty of sun are provided.

One of the best features of bougainvilleas is their marvellous adaptability to training in such a wide variety of different forms. Whether these be quite small bonsai, cascades, espaliers or standards, all can be adapted to container culture. I have seen marvellous specimens in India trailing over balconies from large wooden boxes; a lovely garden in the Philippines features rows of uniform-sized pots along the circular drive leading to the house; and here in Hawaii I know of a potted plant which has grown undisturbed for twenty-five years! This one is in a quite large tub, around 40 cm in diameter, and it is fed regularly, which of course, is important under these conditions. With bougainvilleas it is necessary to feed judiciously, especially in the case of smaller and younger plants. Too much can have the effect of promoting lush leaf growth at the expense of flowers.

An excellent booklet on bougainvilleas distributed by the University of Hawaii advises a light application of organic fertiliser such as dried blood, bone meal, etc., to be given to the plant when it is first planted in a container, followed by a teaspoon of 10-10-10 fertiliser per gallon container every two months after it is established. Additionally, it is advised to spray the plant once a month with a liquid fertiliser containing minor elements.

This booklet suggests as a potting medium equal parts of soil, peat and perlite, a mixture which does not compact, and will ensure the essential drainage, also allowing excess fertiliser to leach out. Some experts here advise a small application of superphosphate given every two months alternating with the feeding of 10-10-10. This is for additional leaf and stem growth. If plants are to be kept small, or in bonsai form, this would not apply as too much growth could be made. Undoubtedly plants grown in containers tend to flower better than those in the ground by reason of the restriction of root growth.

I have found that some varieties will flower continuously if the plants are pruned back immediately after blooming. How much pruning will of course depend upon whether you wish to keep the plant small, but if longer branches are required, then simply cut off the spent flower stems. Heavy pruning is unnecessary for smaller-growing double varieties which tend to make new buds even before the old flowers are spent, but larger singles definitely benefit from fairly heavy pruning.

Where the latter are grown in prominent positions on balconies or patios, it is advisable to have them growing in light plastic pots inside the more decorative containers or troughs so that they can be lifted out and put in the background during this after-bloom period, but be sure that this background position is still one which will receive plenty of sun, for this is more important than ever at this time to ensure that the new growth will produce ample flower buds. I have found that the time taken to make this new growth will vary with different types, and for this reason, if space is limited, it is wise to be very selective in order to have the varieties that will give the longest and most continuous periods of bloom.

Bougainvillea cultivation will be somewhat different in the really tropical regions such as the Philippines where there is a definite 'rainy season'. Fertilis-ing, for instance, would not be a year-round affair as in Hawaii or in the warmer areas of the United States or Australia. Mrs Luisa Perez-Rubio, who achieves magnificent results in her lovely garden in the Philippines, gave me these notes on her cultural methods. 'Fertilise with complete fertiliser as soon as the rainy season is over . . . It is not necessary to mix the fertiliser into the soil. The watering will take care of transporting it down to the roots a little at a time. Repeat the process *after* the plants have bloomed, and you are ready to prune lightly, in preparation for the next blooming cycle, which should start immediately, if given the proper attention. *Do not* fertilise during the rainy season, as even if the plants want to flower, the rains will rot the buds, and this becomes an unnecessary strain for the plant.'

Mrs Perez-Rubio continues, 'It is not necessary to water during the rainy season, unless there is a long spell of two weeks during which there is absolutely no rainfall. Often times the humidity alone is sufficient to keep the plants wet. After the rains have stopped, water once a day. Do not overwater. Just allow enough to keep the plants from drying up. If little water is given, the tendency is for the leaves to fall, which then forces the plant to bring out its blooms. Once the buds show, water generously, even twice a day if weather is hot and dry as this will keep the buds from wilting, as well as prolonging the life of the flowers for a good two weeks. Heavy pruning is done during the rainy season. Prune back all branches leaving about 30 cm of main branches. All small weak secondary growth should be cut off. Repotting is done every three or four years also during the rainy season, when the plant has become too root bound, and little soil remains. Then it is time to cut about 50 per cent off the roots and return to the pot with new soil.'

Gardeners in Bangkok confirm these cultural directions, as climatic conditions are somewhat similar. All agree that bougainvillea is the most decorative and versatile plant for a tropical garden, as it certainly is for subtropical ones.

Propagation is similar in all climates, the simplest method being by cuttings about the thickness of a lead pencil, and about 15 cm long. Remove all but the top two leaves, and plant in either vermiculite, sand, perlite or sand and peat mixed 50/50. Rooting will be hastened if the bases of the cuttings are first dusted with one of the rooting powders, and, if the climate is dry, cover with a plastic bag. When shoots begin to form into leaves, carefully lift the rooted cuttings into separate pots. Care must be taken not to damage the brittle young roots which are not at all strong at the base of new plants. Keep both cuttings and newly planted pots in a shady position, bringing the rooted plants into the sun in about two weeks' time. When strong growth has commenced it is advisable to keep nipping shoots back to form a sturdy, well-branched plant for the first year or so, sacrificing flowers at this stage in order to provide a better framework for later blooms.

Where climates are less warm than in the Philippines, don't follow the foregoing advice as to root-pruning. Where growth is less rapid the removal of half the roots could be too much. I usually cut off around a third depending on the size and strength of the plant. Certainly they make enormously long roots, but if the thought of cutting them alarms you, you can 'pot on' until they are quite large, but shake out all the old soil and give a fresh lot each time.

The question of varieties is a tricky one, sometimes varying from one country to another, but all seem to agree upon 'Mary Palmer'. I've seen it with this name in India, the Philippines, Hong Kong, and the United States. Its popularity is not sur-

prising, as it is the most versatile of all, adapting to so many forms, but although it has a very long (almost continuous) flowering period, the flowers fall very soon. But we cannot have everything!

'Miss Manila' is a lovely salmon shaded orange single, also long flowering, as is 'Yellow Glory', a very strong grower. A marvellous red is 'San Diego Red' which is also a long flowerer. I find the whites less good in this respect, perhaps the best being 'Jamaica White' or 'Snow White'. An absolutely lovely double is 'Bridal Bouquet' opening with pale pink and white flowers which deepen in colour as it ages. I found that 'Scarlet O'Hara' flowered well in my Sydney garden, and it is better suited to pot culture than most. There are several good shades in doubles, but some nurseries are very casual about names, so that they just have to be bought when in flower which, of course, is a good plan anyway.

If you only have space for one bougainvillea, this white single could deserve a place. This is Jamaica White. It needs to be well pruned after flowering to keep it compact.

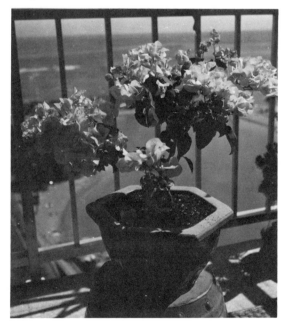

12

The attractive azaleas

I doubt whether spring could ever be really complete without the lovely azaleas! There are azaleas of almost every colour and form, and in such variety that choice becomes difficult indeed for the small-space gardener, but we who garden in the sky must be especially selective here, because it is important to choose not only those with the longest flowering period, but those which will still look reasonably attractive when not in flower. Not for us therefore, the glowing orange, yellows and reds of the deciduous Mollis and Ghent varieties, lovely though their perfume can be; not for us either the evergreen Kurume varieties with their small densely packed early blooms. This mass of colour, lovely though it is, is too short-lived, and this applies to most of the larger-flowered Indicas, which make such beautiful banks of colour in open gardens. However there are varieties and hybrids which combine all the attractions of the Indicas with compactness, excellent length of flowering, and variety and size of bloom for outstripping any of their predecessors.

These 'new hybrids', as they are most often called, are being propagated constantly in the United States, Australia and Europe, and many are descended from the type known as the 'Belgian doubles' (although many of these are actually single). This name describes those originally propagated in Belgium for the florist trade. They appear in the shops in marvellous balls of compact colour in earliest spring and late winter, some even being forced, with modern methods, into flower early. They last well indoors, and in protected places on balconies when weather is not severe.

Quite often, in the colder climates, they are treated as are the Christmas poinsettias, that is, relegated to the trash can at the end of their flowering, primarily because subsequent care becomes a problem if insufficient space is available, but in moderate climates they should be treasured and encouraged to continue flowering by cutting off spent flowers as they fade, kept well watered and given small doses of special azalea and rhododendron food whilst keeping them outdoors in broken sunlight, if possible. Some types will take more shade than others, but for new buds, some sun and good light are necessary. For those with clusters of flowers, it will help if not only the spent flowers are removed, but also a section of the stem below the clusters. This will not only help to keep the plant compact, but will force new growth along the remaining part of the stem, which will, in turn, carry later buds.

I have, when gardening in a temperate climate, been able to keep azaleas of this variety in flower from mid-winter until late summer. These were all in pots. Most of these were large flowered semi-doubles, the longest flowering being 'Paul Schame', 'Eri' (or 'Eri Schame'), 'Countess de Kerchove', 'Avenir', 'Pink Ruffles', 'Red Ruffles' and the lovely white 'Deutsche Perle'. Most of these are old, well-known favourites, but there are many others, and many newer descendants of all of these. Then there are many hybrids and crosses with these, and other varieties, some with smaller, double flowers such as the lovely 'Sweetheart Supreme', 'Azama Kagami', and a host of others, many also long-flowering. Look around your local nursery in spring, asking which types will do best in your district, and try out a few small plants to see how they like your conditions. The 100-mm pot size will take up very little space and will have enough flowers to justify its being kept indoors in place of cut flowers, where the flowers will last well if it is given a good light, preferably near a window. If kept out on the balcony, give them a shady place whilst in bloom as flowers then will last longer, especially if protected from wind. When the flowers are cut back, the plants need some sun and feeding.

One of the loveliest things about azaleas is their adaptability to being changed to more decorative pots even while in full flower, and this can be an advantage if you want to have them in the living room for a time, and the nursery or chain-store pot is ugly. Do not overpot them; they will remain in a small size for several years, but they do like fairly shallow containers, as their roots are spreading, but not deep. For this reason, they lend themselves very well to being grown as bonsai, or to being shaped in a number of different ways. Unless you are experienced, or somewhat of a gambler, however, try to do your shaping with a minimum of wiring, because the stems are extremely brittle, and you will be quite likely to hear a horri-

Azalea 'Deutche Perle' has been popular for many years. A double white with a lime-green centre, this is a good container variety.

ble 'snap' on a formerly promising branch if you treat them as you would a more pliable pine. Better to rely on clipping to the desired shape, and bend branches down gently with small lead weights or tie them to a wire beneath the rim of the pot.

The type most often used for bonsai culture is the Satsuki, the native Japanese variety, also known as Macrantha type. These are winter-hardy, and bloom later than most others, and here too, many late hybrids have been introduced, among them the dainty, small-growing 'Gumpo', ideal for confined spaces, but with a shorter period of bloom than the Belgian types. Some of the newer ones have very large flowers, often mottled and prettily variegated, but there are lovely plain colours too.

When you do need to pot on, be sure to use an acid soil, as lime in any form is anathema to azaleas. I have often used pure peat moss if it is good quality, but it must be thoroughly soaked first. There is usually no difficulty in getting packaged azalea-daphne mixtures, or lime-free leaf

This is a five-year-old cumquat, an excellent little tree for a limited space. Decorative all year round, even when not bearing fruit, cumquats will grow in all but the very coldest climates. When winters are really severe, they can be taken indoors where they will make a most attractive indoor plant if given a place in a good light.

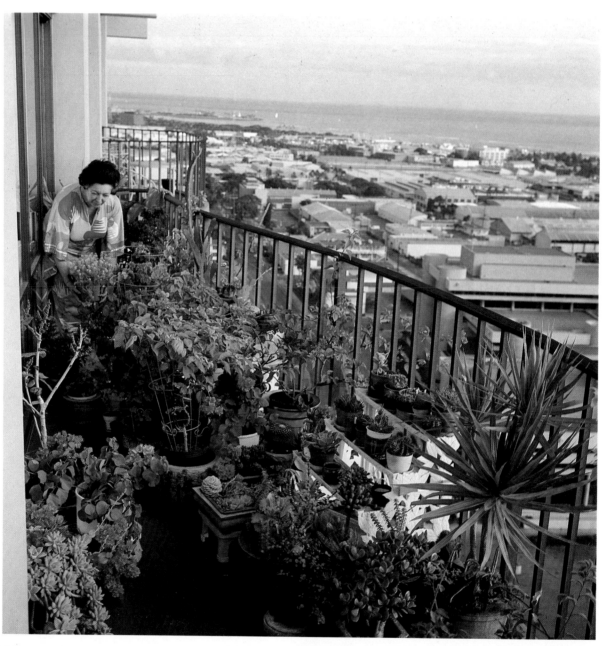

This photo shows how well a garden can grow even on the twenty-seventh floor of a quite windy location. The big variety of plants includes bougainvilleas, geraniums, various succulents, annuals, palms, and even edible fig. (Photograph by Robert Ebert.)

Despite a great deal of wind, geraniums flourish on this balcony garden.

This assortment of vegetables on one side of a penthouse garden provides excellent proof that one can have a kitchen garden on the sixteenth floor.

This collection of vegetables is ample evidence of the variety that can be grown in a not very large area. Full sun is needed for most of these.

Hibiscus and bougainvilleas blend well together here.

mould is good, or even a mulch of this, which will help keep the soil moist, as this is important. They should not be allowed to dry out, but care must also be taken that they are not left standing in water or the soil allowed to remain sodden. Good drainage and a layer of sphagnum moss on the surface will help also, failing the mulch of leaf mould. Do not give them poultry manure. It will be too alkaline. They are not heavy feeders, and even special azalea fertiliser should be given sparingly, just after flowering.

Watch out for thrip, red spider mites, or

The lovely azalea 'Azuma Kagami' has a very long flowering season and a graceful habit of growth.

These azaleas enjoy the protection of a semi-enclosed balcony, where sliding glass windows break the force of the wind. An outside shelf gives useful added space.

lacebug, which will settle in under the leaves, but can be kept at bay with regular spraying under the leaves and overhead (but preferably not whilst in bloom). At the first sign of any of these pests spray with soapy water, followed 15 minutes later by clear water, but if this is not effective and you feel you *must* use a pesticide, let it be malathion. 'House and garden' type sprays would also be suitable, but *never* use ordinary household sprays for plants.

13

The elegant camellias

Possibly the ideal all-round plant for temperate and cold-climate balconies would be the beautiful and increasingly popular *Camellia japonica*. I specify *japonica* because the fast-growing *C. sasanqua* type, although very attractive for pot or tub culture, would eventually outgrow even quite large containers, whereas the japonicas come in many dwarf and semi-dwarf forms and have the added advantage of holding their blooms for longer periods than the earlier-flowering sasanquas, whose flowers tend to shatter and fall within a day or so. The fallen flowers of this prolific variety usually make a very pretty carpet beneath the plants, but whilst this is attractive in the open garden, it could be a distinct drawback on a balcony!

So enormous is the range of forms, colours and types of *C. japonica* that it becomes difficult to know which to recommend from among the bewildering crop of new hybrids, sports, and seedlings being raised every year. They become larger and more durable each year, yet many of the old favourites are still able to hold their own, and continue to be much loved and widely grown.

It is however important, before making any choice, to consider carefully the place where your camellias are to be grown, not only from the point of view of aspect, but from that of the place they are to occupy in what will almost certainly be a limited space. That is to say, if you wish to train them against a wall espalier fashion, it will obviously be best to choose plants with a tall spreading habit. If they are to occupy a pot or tub near the front of your balcony, you need a more compact type which will not become too wide. Most established camellia specialist nurseries issue a catalogue giving details of habit and speed of growth along with descriptions of colour and form, so try to get all this information rather than selecting from the very tempting displays of blooms to be found at camellia shows and in plant shops. Speed of growth is important too. It is better to settle for the slower-growing varieties, assuming that you are able to start off with a reasonably sized specimen, rather than to find yourself with a beautiful, large plant which has outgrown its surroundings in a few years, because, contrary to popular belief, many of the camellias, especially the newer varieties, can grow quite quickly. The lovely reticulatas, for instance, have very wide-spreading branches which make them suitable only for the open garden, or possibly roomy patio locations. Many nurseries also have notes in their catalogues as to which varieties are best suited for pot or tub culture. So arm yourself with this information, and *then* sally forth to the flower shows to look at the blooms on display.

If you are lucky enough to have a fairly large area of wall, nothing could be more attractive than an espaliered camellia, and the number suitable for this purpose is enormous. See chapter 2 on containers for suitable ones, such as the large rectangular plastic wastepaper holder, a square tub or a trough. A camellia could grow in one of these for quite a few years as they actually have quite a small root system in relation to their top growth, and as with most potted plants it is better for the roots to be a little crowded than to have too much unoccupied soil around them. This soil eventually becomes stagnant and this naturally has a bad effect on the plant. I find it better to pot them on into progressively larger sizes, giving new rich soil with each potting.

The tall compact varieties are good for either free-standing positions or for growing in individual pots also against a wall if you feel that one spreading espaliered plant occupies space that you would rather give to several different ones. For corner positions these are also good, as are the lower-growing compact types which look very attractive trimmed into either dome, ball, or cone shapes, such as one sees in formal French and Italian gardens. These are decorative even when not in flower because their glossy green leaves are attractive all year round. For this reason too, these amiable plants can be put to work to provide a living screen if you need more privacy or have an unattractive area to hide, or even to help break the wind where railings are too open.

In such cases it will not take very long to increase the density of your screen by trimming back the shoots coming out at the front of the plants, thus stimulating the needed side growths. As these plants continue to grow for much of the year, this trimming can continue right up till the time for the buds to appear, and you will naturally desist from then until the flowering period ends, when it will be time to make any major corrections in shape or to remove larger branches if this becomes necessary. The same method should be followed in the case of the formal compact shapes, maintaining the desired shape by nipping unwanted shoots as soon as they appear rather than waiting until they grow into long stems.

An important consideration in making the choice of varieties is also that of your aspect. Some types, for instance, will stand more sun than others. This usually applies to the reds, most of which will take more sun than pale pinks or whites which will burn far more than, for instance, the old favourite red, 'Czar'. Even 'Czar' will give better blooms in partial shade than in full sun, where both flowers and foliage will burn if it becomes too hot. My namesake, 'Margaret Davis', a consistent prize-winner in both Australia and many areas of the United States, is remarkably sun-hardy, although it is white-edged pink. Salmon pink 'Hana Fuki', pale pink 'Cho Cho San' and pink and white 'Lady Loch' will also take quite a lot of sun. All of these are equally good in shade or semi-shade. Sometimes reflected heat from a white wall will have a bad effect, so keep in mind that these are shade-loving plants, preferring the type of conditions provided by protection from overhanging trees. A difficult requirement certainly, for balcony locations, but not an impossible one to simulate with a little determination. See chapter 8 on trees for balconies for suggestions, and also consider vines suitable for providing shade.

The platforms mounted on small casters can be very useful for camellias, in order to move them around according to the shifting position of the sun at various seasons. Even with this kind of attention unfortunately it is just not possible to grow camellias in really hot climates. Even in the relatively mild Hawaiian climate they refuse to grow except in elevated locations or the moist valleys, and only achieve moderately presentable blooms at around 1 000 metres or higher on the slopes of the volcanos on Maui and the Big Island of Hawaii. We grew some varieties quite well in our sea-level garden in Sydney, but those in our 1 000 metre-high mountain garden where winters are very cold produced far better and bigger blooms.

It would be worth while to check which types seem to thrive best in your own neighbourhood also before making the final choice. This careful selection in cases where only a few plants can be accommodated will pay off in the long run because these are very long-lived plants, and it would be a pity to spend several years training your plants to good shapes only to find that they do not give good flowers.

Camellias need a slightly acid soil with a good deal of leaf mould or peat moss. It may be possible to buy special camellia soil from local nurseries or garden shops, and many firms package special fertilisers. These should be used sparingly as soon as there is any sign of growth, particularly just after flowering, but remember that amounts shown on the packages should be halved for container-grown plants. This applies to most plants. A good fertiliser is the slow-release Osmacote.

Good drainage is important as frequent watering will possibly be needed under balcony conditions to keep the plants fairly moist, which they should be at all times especially when flowers and buds are forming, but do not leave them with 'wet feet' that is, an accumulation of water in the saucers beneath the pot. Do not water until the soil surface is dry. In very hot weather it would be wise to spray the foliage in the late afternoon when there is no danger of sun reaching the leaves. I give most of my plants a daily spraying to

Choose your camellias to suit the spot you have in mind for them. Near the front of a balcony you will need a compact type that will not become too wide.

keep the dust off the leaves in any case, doing this usually at night, but this may be best done earlier in cold climates. Most japonicas will stand temperatures down to 3ºC (37ºF) but this would be too cold for the completely double flowers which will need to be moved to a protected place in very cold winters.

When transferring a newly bought plant from its nursery can or plastic pot to an ornamental container take care not to cover the roots too deeply. They should be no more than 2-3 cm below the soil level, as they need a certain amount of air. A light mulch of sphagnum moss, manure or leaf mould will help to conserve moisture provided it is not too deep.

One of the greatest advantages of camellias is their freedom from the many pests and diseases that plague most other plants. Occasionally they may be attacked by scale and mites. Use an oil spray for the scale and either Kelthane or Malathion for mites but only use these when it is really necessary. Indiscriminate spraying could destroy valuable predators such as ladybugs or any birds you may be lucky enough to have, in addition to being unpleasant and (if not handled carefully) dangerous to the sprayer.

Die-back is a disease that can attack camellias in certain areas. This is very hard to control, although I have some growers say that they found Benlate helpful. As this is a disease that will travel quickly throughout the plant, it is advisable to cut off the affected part immediately, and to cut the stem back to where there is no more sign of the tell-tale brown in the centre of the stem. It is recognised by a sudden collapse and drooping usually of new growths.

Did you know that fallen blooms that are in good condition can be kept for quite a few days in the crisper of your refrigerator? In this way they can be saved for table decoration, as one is naturally very reluctant to cut flowers from precious decorative plants.

Milton Brown of the American Camellia Society has suggested that it would be important in cold areas where temperature goes below about –2ºC (28ºF) to have large plants on casters or wheeled platforms so as to wheel them indoors on these very cold nights. They can then be wheeled out to the open air the next day, or when the temperature rises again. Because the dry heat of the average apartment would not suit these plants, it is suggested that those fortunate enough to have an unheated spare room or bathroom with sufficient light or equipped with a Gro-lux lamp might use this for temporary shelter. Confirming the feasibility of growing camellias indoors, another member of this Society, Mrs Pat Walton successfully grew and flowered camellias in a basement equipped with fluorescent lighting in Augusta, Georgia, and later in New Jersey, in a basement with a thermopane door on the south side, which enabled the plants to receive sun all morning. The basement has a hot-water heating system which maintains the temperature at 10 to 13ºC (50 to 55ºF) throughout the winter and the humidity remains high at all times. This indoor situation has enabled Mrs Walton to avoid all insect and disease problems, and so successful has it been that she plans to leave the plants in the basement all summer.

As Mrs Walton's plants are not large, she is able to bring them into the house when they are in bloom, and not one of her plants failed to bloom in the past season! Well, it could certainly be worth the cold-climate apartment dweller's while to take a look at the basement of his building for unused, or unfrequented space, if he longs to grow these very beautiful flowers! Some apartments even have reasonably large storerooms which could be possibly pressed into service, especially those with only wide-meshed wire divisions, which can be locked. A house, of course, has many more possibilities.

A suggestion on the matter of disbudding, which many varieties need, even in small plants. The usual tendency is to remove all the smallest buds, keeping just one or two of the biggest. Instead, if you keep also one of the smaller ones, it will give you a flower after the others have finished, and if this is done with all plants, a longer flowering period will result.

14

The wonderful citrus family

No matter how small your balcony, you could grow at least one citrus tree, for this very large family includes specimens from just a few centimetres high to 3 to 5 metres. Even the larger members can be often found in dwarf forms. I doubt whether any tree is more decorative or rewarding to grow. Even if the fruit were not edible, the tree would be worth growing for its beauty. A well-grown, well-shaped citrus tree can outshine even the most glamorous of flowering plants. I am reminded as I write of how this was demonstrated to me during the time when we had a beautiful garden in Sydney which was 'opened for inspection' in aid of various charities each spring. Day after day admiring crowds stood around the collection of citrus trees on the terrace, and although there were many lovely azaleas, rhododendrons, camellias and magnolias, it was the potted citrus trees which constantly stole the show. We were always on hand to answer questions on these occasions, and the question we were most often asked was 'How can we grow oranges, lemons and mandarins in tubs like yours?'

So now I am going to tell *you,* because I know that whichever type of citrus you may decide to try, it will bring you an enormous amount of pleasure for many years. Yes, *many* years, for even on a balcony these trees can be kept in even quite small pots for very long periods. Bonsai growers will confirm this, but if you prefer something not quite so small, and have room for a tub, you can plan on a lifetime tree. I was once fortunate enough to spend some time in Paris with the Director of the parks and gardens of that lovely city, and as his territory included the gardens of Versailles, I asked about the age of the orange trees in those big square tubs that some of you may have seen. It seems that some of these are still the original trees planted at the order of Louis XIV, the 'Sun King'. They would, I imagine, have often been root pruned and given fresh soil in all the years between, and also would have been moved into a conservatory or 'orangery' for the winter months, as is done with the citrus trees so much used in the lovely formal gardens in Italy. An Italian gardener once told me that this is why the decorative Italian tubs are so often equipped with handles, to make it easier to lift them indoors. In England, we still see in some of the lovely old gardens conservatory-like structures known as 'orangeries', even though they will probably be occupied by other plants.

Do not despair if yours is a cold climate and you do not have an orangery, as your plants can spend winters right in the house serving as decorative house plants. You must give them a good light, as close as possible to a window, and keep them well watered to offset the drying effects of heating. A bowl of water close by will also help provide the needed humidity. I know a lady who keeps a lovely cumquat in a tub in her living room permanently, but it is right inside wide doors leading to a terrace, and these doors are open much of the day.

It will naturally be much simpler in cases where they must be moved indoors in winter to have fairly small plants, and even if your local nursery does not stock the grafted dwarf types, it is still possible to grow the very attractive little Calamondin which has different names in different countries. In the Philippines it is Calamanci, in England its botanical name is *Citrus mitis*. By any name, it is a beautiful little tree with small orange-like fruit and fragrant waxy flowers. Then in the slightly larger category comes the myrtle-leaved mandarin (Chinoti) with smaller flowers growing in clusters all the way along the stems, and fruit, also in clusters, that stays on the tree for months. This fruit is not so good for eating as the others, but it is so decorative that I could not imagine anyone wanting to pick it anyway. This tree is so lovely in flower that it would be worth growing just for its flowers. One must search for short plants of this one, as it tends to get a stiffly erect habit if not pruned and shaped before this happens.

There are several varieties of cumquat (or kumquat) and these too can be kept quite small. The one which has oval fruit ('Nagami') makes delicious eating picked right from the tree, but the round-fruited one ('Marumi') is quite bitter, although it makes very good preserves and marmalade. The beauty of cumquat fruit is that it can be left on the tree for many weeks and cut and used only when it becomes obvious that it is too ripe to remain any longer. There are also variegated-leaved forms of both these cumquats to be found, but with these much of the attraction of the contrast between the bright fruit and the glossy dark green leaves is lost.

If you prefer the idea of growing oranges, lemons, limes, tangerines or mandarins and cannot accommodate large trees, go to a specialist nursery and walk along the rows of trees in search of one that has been grafted low down, or even a short tree on a normal graft. Make sure that the stem is straight however, because that is necessary if you are going to grow it with a bushy top.

Even if you plan to grow it against a wall, espalier fashion, you should start off with a good straight stem. Citrus of all kinds lend themselves beautifully to this form of growth. If you have a sunny wall, plant your tree in a square tub, or alternatively a deep trough. In either case it will be possible to attach a small trellis or some crossed stakes to give support if it is difficult to plug the wall. The purpose here is not so much to give support, because the branches are quite strong, but to train the tree into an attractive shape. Also one of the reasons for growing trees against sunny walls is to give them the maximum of precious sun and warmth, just as it is where they are grown in gardens in many countries where winters are cold and summers short.

Lemons, although not always easy to train into formal shapes, will make excellent espaliers. The Meyer lemon, that not-too-sour lemon with orange in its parentage, is an excellent variety to grow in either temperate or cold climates. Some that we grew in our cold mountain garden at 1 000 metres sailed right through frosts and snow out in the open ground, so I feel sure they would do so on a sheltered balcony. Cumquats too, seem to thrive in a wide range of climates. Oranges can be more choosey, depending on variety; it is best to consult your local nursery on this. And do try to get, if you can, that most beautifully coloured of all the citrus, the tangelo, a marvellous orange-red, and a cross between a mandarin and a grapefruit. About the size of a fairly medium orange, these highly decorative fruit remain on the tree for long periods. Taste varies somewhat according to the district and soil in which they are grown, but they are less sweet than their mandarin parent, and are very good for refreshing drinks. There are several types of tangelo, one round like an orange, another more pear-shaped, but all are good.

Mandarins and tangerines are worth investigating. Choose the variety best suited to your climate and district. There are many varieties, and it is important to try for those with the best fruiting record. This can vary quite a lot too. Although grapefruit grow beautifully in tubs, unless you have a good-sized terrace, it may be best to forego these.

If possible try to buy your tree in a plastic pot. These are so much easier to deal with than the metal cans often used by nurseries. Better still, of course if it is in a sufficiently good-looking container already, or if you merely plan to place the pot inside a decorative planter. As citrus trees do not have very large root systems, the soil in which the tree is bought should be adequate for at least three years, provided that you give regular applications of fertiliser. Most stores now carry special citrus food and this should be sufficient if you carefully follow directions on the box. Do remember that these will be for trees in open ground unless specified otherwise, and amounts should be halved, as they should always be for things growing in pots. You can also give applications more often in this case, however, as nutrients do leach out with the more frequent watering needed for pots. Poultry manure given in late winter and autumn is very good also.

If your tree is bought from open ground, that is, bare-rooted, take great care that the roots are not allowed to dry out while

Ideal for balconies with a reasonable amount of sun is the colourful little Chinoti or myrtle-leaved mandarin. This is a slow-growing tree which stays quite small and is ideal for pot culture. The flowers are fragrant and are borne along the branches, making a lovely spring display. The fruit is mainly decorative and remains on the tree for many months.

preparing the container. Keep them soaking in water at this time. Be sure to provide good drainage in the container by putting a curved crock or piece of broken crockery (convex side up) over the hole. You should always keep any broken cups or saucers for this purpose. Put several more pieces around the first one, and then cover these with some coarse material such as pieces of sacking, net, open bark, anything porous enough to let the water through, but prevent soil running out. Hair trimmings are fine, and most beneficial to plants. Now fill in some soil (the richest you can get but alkaline). I always prefer to spend the extra amount for good-quality, sterilised potting soil rather than to attempt the very messy business of trying to mix and sterilise soils in confined balcony space.

It must be emphasised here that the pots for these bare-root trees should be just large enough to accommodate the

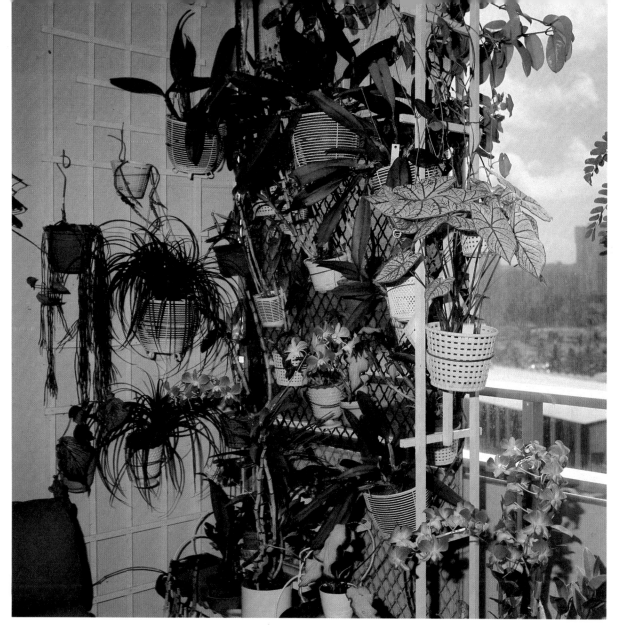

This garden arch provides space for quite a number of plants which could not otherwise be accommodated. The trellis on the wall provides support for one end of the top section.

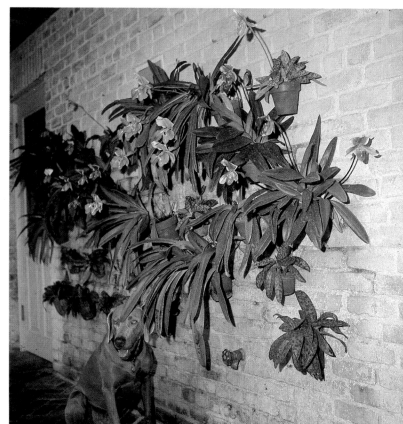

An effective use of wall space is shown here. Cold climate dwellers could emulate this beautifully with pots of polyanthus spring bulbs, or an assortment of summer annuals. The pots are held by clamps on their rims which hook to rings driven into plugs in the brick wall.

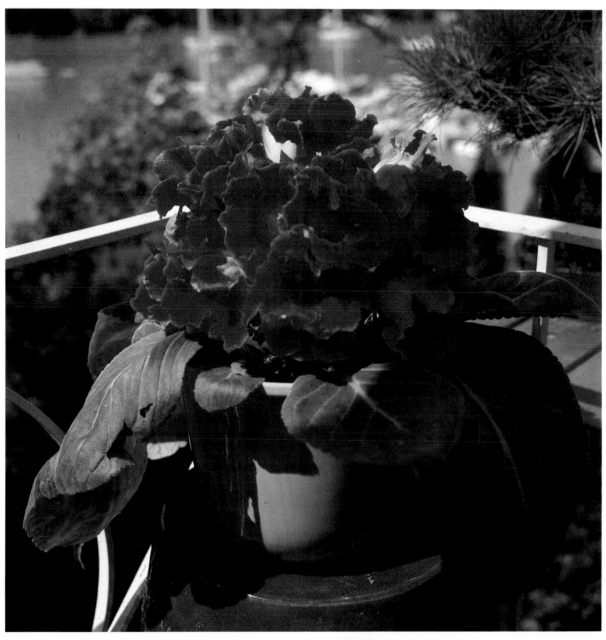

The lovely gloxinias are good for sheltered balconies, given an hour or two of morning sun. One can either buy them already in flower, or, if you have a lot of patience, a wonderful assortment can be raised from seed. The tubers will continue to flower for several years if dried off each winter. (Photograph above by Sir Kenneth Fung.)

roots, and they should be planted at the same depth as they were in the soil of the nursery. Over-potting of any plant is very bad. The unused soil rapidly becomes stagnant, holding too much water, and roots can rot rapidly under these conditions. It is better to repot more often than to pot plants in too-large containers in the belief that they will 'grow into' them. This is one of the most common mistakes of inexperienced gardeners, who believe that they are being kind to their plants in giving them plenty of room! Make sure that the newly planted tree has plenty of water. When using new soil I always let the plant stand in a saucer of water for half a day to be sure the soil becomes properly moistened.

Citrus trees from open ground usually have three main branches. Treatment of these will depend, at this stage, on the shape you wish the tree to ultimately take. If it is to be spread against the wall, in either a formal or informal espalier, tie them to their supports, nip out the top of the central, upright branch to induce side shoots, and tie the others almost horizontally. Do not tie these too tightly; remember to leave room for growth. As your space will probably not permit the height or length of the perfect 'ladder' types seen in open gardens, it could be best to try not to be too rigid about this. Think in terms of either a fan shape, or an informal spreading form. When side branches appear they should also be loosely tied to the supports when long enough. Nip out those not needed to maintain the shape you are aiming for. This should be done before they become long, of course.

When the desired main framework has been achieved, it simply becomes a matter of nipping back shoots which tend to grow outwards. If space on your balcony is limited, you may have to be somewhat ruthless about this, in order to keep a very 'flattened' tree, but it will keep it neat and you can still leave enough length to carry some leaves, and hopefully some buds.

I know some gardeners who are very strict in their training of the original espalier shapes, even to the extent of starting with just one stem, which is cut back from the usual height of around 75 cm to 30 cm which, although ultimately giving a better formal shape, sets the tree back at least a year. Whilst this would not matter so much when it is occupying a background place in the open garden, it would not look at all attractive in the close confines of a balcony. You should aim here for quick, even if less meticulous results.

It is possible to achieve quite a good compromise between a conventional espalier and the European round-top ideal by aiming at a flattened type of the latter; that is, keep the tree to a single stem, but instead of having a fully round top, one side stays flat against the wall and the rest is kept rounded in the usual way. This can be very effective against a white wall, and results are quicker, not only as a result of the warmth of the wall, but because all growth is concentrated toward the front giving a more bushy effect. Space is also saved, of course. For this, or the normally all-round shape, it is simply a matter of keeping the stem as straight as possible, using a stake if necessary in the early stages, then nipping out the shoots when the desired height is reached and keeping the subsequent side shoots nipped when they reach the shape you are aiming for. Do not be too severe about this when it is time for buds to appear, for after all, who wants to spoil the joy of those lovely fragrant blossoms, which would justify your tree's existence even if they were not followed by beautiful fruit! Just shelve the matter of shaping at this time; it can easily be resumed later.

Unfortunately, gardening in the sky does not confer immunity from pests, and it is possible that the scale and aphis which plague trees on the ground could follow them aloft. How this happens, I have never been able to discover; perhaps the eggs are already there, or are carried in with other plants, but come they do. However, we do have a great advantage in being able to check our plants at close quarters, and both these pests are easy to beat if dealt with early. In the case of scale, whether it be white or brown, as soon as you see the first sign rub it off with any fairly firm brush. An old toothbrush kept on hand for this purpose should take care of it. The brown type, not so easy to spot as the white, usually clusters on the main stem. The white, which is softer and has a waxy look, will be found on the smaller branches or at the base of leaves.

For aphis (or greenfly) the favourite spots are the tips of new shoots. For these, spray with soapy water, or dip the branch into a bowl of soapy water to wash them off. If you cannot dip them (the branch may not be flexible enough) then spray them, leaving the soapy water on for no more than 15 minutes. Then spray again with clean water; it is not good for young growth to be left for too long. Above all, do not dash for the can of pesticide at the first sign of an insect. Remember that even the most allegedly harmless of these products can often have cumulative adverse effects when used in confined spaces, and are either inhaled, or absorbed through the skin. See chapter 20 on this.

Remember too, that many of these pests, especially the beastly mealy bug, are conveyed to your plants by ants, those most pesky of insects to plague balcony and indoor gardeners. If you can banish these, much trouble can be avoided. Again, try the old-fashioned methods first. Slower but safer! If you happen to see a black sooty mould, this will be a forerunner to scale, to which it is allied.

Calamondin *(Citrus mitis)* is a wonderful miniature member of the citrus family which is ideal for pot culture and for growing as a bonsai. It will hold its orange-coloured fruits for a long time. Also it has the advantage of growing well in many different climates.

Use the soapy water treatment, or scrub it off at the first sign.

It is difficult to lay down rules for watering citrus. As with any plant, this will depend entirely upon the location, rainfall and time of year, but it would be safe to say that in their growing period, these trees need to be kept reasonably well watered; that is, watered when the soil on the surface seems dry, but not if it is already moist, or if there is any water in the saucer beneath the pot. Like most balcony plants, they appreciate a nightly spraying, or, if weather is cool, spray in the afternoon after the sun has left them. This will help greatly for general health, and keep the leaves glossy and free from dust.

15

Climbing plants

Climbing or trailing plants can be used to good effect even on quite small balconies. Any wall becomes far more attractive when used as a background for leaves and flowers, and a surprising number of vines adapt very well to being grown in containers provided that sufficient support can be given.

The question of plugging walls to provide this necessary support can be a tricky one if you are not the owner of your apartment or house. If the owner is unwilling to give permission for this, you can use those small adhesive hooks often used to hold small pictures on indoor walls. These can support wires, string, or even a small lightweight trellis of wire or plastic. Also a series of strings (or a fine nylon cord, which looks better) can be tied around the pot in which the plant is growing and linked to some small hooks where the walls join the ceiling to provide support for a vine. With luck, there might even be a wood beading there.

If you have an ugly view to shut out, or need more privacy, then a length of wire netting with as open a mesh as possible would perhaps be the best. There is no limit to the variety of vines which can then be grown. Do not choose those with a very thick growth habit which could exclude the light from the rooms beyond, or from the rest of your balcony. There are many suitable vines which can be easily kept under control; the choice depends, of course, on your climate.

Possibly the best all-round vine for this type of wire-mesh screen would be ivy. It can now be found in many forms, from the well-known old English type through to some with quite tiny leaves. A very quick-growing one is *Hedera* 'Holly', with attractively waved somewhat holly-like leaves. Ivies are best grown on wire rather than against a balcony wall because their tightly clinging roots will leave unsightly marks if they are later removed. Also their tenacious habit of delving into any gaps in plaster or brickwork can become quite troublesome.

There is a very attractive semi-climbing cross between ivy and *Fatsia* known as *Fatshedera*. With the strong stems of its *Fatsia* parent it requires little support. From the *Fatsia* parent also come the large glossy leaves, for which this plant is so greatly prized. In Japan *Fatsia japonica* appears in almost every garden. From both parents *Fatshedera* inherits great hardiness. It can be used outdoors or as a decorative indoor plant. Whilst it is adaptable to either sunny or shaded locations, its handsome leaves show to better advantage in shade. *Fatsia,* ivy and *Fatshedera* are not difficult to please regarding soil, but prefer a fairly rich loamy compost.

Another well-known plant is the handsome *Monstera deliciosa*. Often grown as a non-climbing plant, it will nevertheless reach any height required if given a wall or any strong support to which its thick aerial roots can cling. These aerial roots cause some concern to gardeners, especially as this plant does seem to produce many more than are needed to help it climb, and as they tend to push out rather untidily the question is often asked whether they can be cut off without damage to the plant. Shortening a few does no harm, but wherever possible guide them down into the soil of the pot. Even when they are quite tall, this can still be done as these roots reach a great length. They actually take nourishment from the air, but for pot-grown plants where they are receiving periodical fertiliser, this is not as essential to their wellbeing as when they are clinging to the trees in their native habitat.

The range of philodendrons is enormous, encompassing many larger types down through intermediate sizes to the ever-popular little *P. scandens,* with its appealing heart-shaped leaves and its great adaptability to either climbing upwards or drooping gracefully down from hanging baskets or from pots on high shelves. One of the most attractive uses to which I have seen this plant put was in the penthouse living room of Mr Stewart Mott, where it grew from the walls right across the ceiling, making a beautiful pattern. The branches, which will not cling unaided to smooth surfaces, were held to the walls and ceiling in this case by small strips of white adhesive tape such as are used to hold small pictures. This little plant also blends very well with driftwood, as its leaves are small enough not to obscure an attractive piece of wood. It must be remembered that this variety will not tolerate a great deal of sun but on a shaded or semi-shaded balcony it can look beautiful adorning walls or even reaching across the ceiling.

For sunnier balconies there are many lovely vines, both flowering and foliage types, and one can even hope to pick fruit if space permits a grapevine! Even without their delicious fruit, grapevines are very attractive, and if your balcony is too hot in summer, the leaves will provide welcome shade, as they do in the little outdoor cafes which one sees so often in Italy. Italian balconies too, make a lot of use of grapevines, often twining around ancient fluted columns and over lattice shelters. There are other forms of grapevine, equally attractive, grown just for their foliage which colours marvellously in autumn. There is also the similar and very decorative Virginia creeper, ideal for clinging to walls and supports. Another New York penthouse uses this vine to completely clothe the walls of the apartment, creating a lovely cool green background for the hot summers. Ivy geraniums planted in a trough against the railing will clamber up and along the railings for quite a long distance, providing attractive cover.

Possibly the loveliest of all the flowering vines suitable for growing in pots is *Clematis* spp. with its large elegant flowers in many colours. Anyone lucky enough to visit the English Chelsea Flower Show cannot fail to remember the displays of these lovely flowers, in a wonderful range of shades, growing in not-very-large pots. As most varieties are best cut back in winter, there is no problem with the somewhat straggly branches when bare. *Clematis* prefers an alkaline soil, and likes to have its roots in shade, but its branches in sun. It is only suitable for the cooler areas. Sometimes the smaller-flowered types will grow in temperate regions, but it is happiest where winters are cold.

Wisteria, that beautiful giant among climbers can certainly be grown on a balcony. I have seen beautiful specimens flowering in high apartments in southern France and in Italy, usually planted in antique-looking tall 'Aladdin-type' jars. Possibly these containers give the roots a good depth of soil, but repotting these plants could be very tricky, as anyone who has tried to extract a plant from a container with an incurving top will know. Wisteria does need quite frequent repotting, and root pruning, because it is an extremely robust subject. It would be possible, as the roots would have to be cut anyway at this time, to run a very long sharp knife around the top edge of the jar and then drag the plant out and prune away more roots from the base.

When root pruning, about a third should be cut away altogether. Cut an equal amount from the branches to compensate for the reduced root system. Shake off as much as possible of the old soil and replant in fresh rich soil. Deep, straight-sided containers or urns are very suitable for wisteria; or you could use a barrel cut about two-thirds or three-quarters up, and the space around the vine could be filled with flowering annuals or bulbs. Wisteria will flower well in even a small container, but it can sometimes be unpredictable under these conditions: I had to wait 6 or 7 years for one of mine to start flowering, and the Japanese types can sometimes take longer than the commoner Chinese variety. It is best to go to a nursery and buy plants already in bud to avoid this long wait. These will most likely be grafted plants; those grown from suckers, cuttings and seedlings can be very slow in flowering. Full sun is essential for this vine, and it needs a cold or temperate climate.

However, those who live in the tropics have compensations in the lovely fragrant stephanotis and hoyas, and the glamorous night-flowering cereus. All are fast-growing, fragrant and grow well in pots. Stephanotis likes a sunny location, but can grow quite well with only partial sun. Unfortunately it is subject to attacks by mealy bug. Spray periodically with soapy water, being sure to follow this with a spray with clear water no more than 15 minutes later. Do not leave soap on plants very long. If the mealy bug is only fairly sparse, you may only have to use plain water, but once ensconced, stronger measures are needed. Stephanotis performs best if cut back quite hard after flowering is finished.

Hoya obtusifolia has a flower quite similar to that of stephanotis, but its leaves are larger, glossier, round and quite decorative. This vine appears to grow as well in water as in soil; this allows for a wide choice of containers. A piece of charcoal must be kept in the water at all times. Although it will flower quite reasonably well under these conditions, over a long period, soil probably would promote better growth. This vine will grow quite well in shade or sun. It appears to be quite impartial in this respect, which certainly makes it a treasure. Another great plus is that it seems to be resistant to attacks by pests.

There are many other varieties of *Hoya,* perhaps the best known being the medium-flowered *Hoya carnosa,* with pinkish-beige flowers and either plain green or variegated leaves. This one grows in a wide range of climates. This does not grow as rapidly as *H. obtusifolia,* but is very hardy and useful. However it will not stand frost. When the pretty porcelain-like flowers appear you must not yield to the temptation to pick them if you hope for more flowers next year, because this plant has the strange habit of bearing its subsequent flowers in exactly the same places.

So do not remove spent flower stems, as you would with so many other plants. Likewise, pruning is not advised.

Another variety of this attractive *Hoya* genus is the quite small, pendulous *H. bella.* Unlike the larger relatives this one does not grow upwards, but prefers to hang down, making it an ideal hanging basket subject. The stems are very soft and the flowers similar to other hoyas in form and fragrance, but these, and the leaves, are much smaller. Hoya is often known as 'wax plant' for its unusually wax-like texture. It likes a rich soil, but will not need frequent re-potting; in fact, this should only be done when absolutely necessary as the roots tend to resent disturbance.

Clerodendron thomsonae, often called the bleeding heart vine, is another very decorative climbing plant suitable for balcony culture in warm, frost-free areas.

It has clusters of white calyces; small blood-red flowers hang from the centres of these. Unlike the twining plants just described, *C. thomsonae* has quite strong stems which can be kept short enough to grow it as a compact shrubby plant, but it will obligingly grow taller if given some support. There are other clerodendrons, but this one is perhaps most suited to pot culture. The others are quite robust subjects and require quite hot conditions.

If you have a brick wall which you would like to cover with green, it would be hard to surpass the climbing member of the tough *Ficus* genus, *F. pumila*. This quite small-leaved and very attractive little fig will do the job very quickly. No wires, strings, or sticky-tape is needed to hold this little plant in place. It has extremely tenacious sucker-equipped stems which will cling unaided no matter how high the wall, and as yours will not be very high at all, the branches will proceed to meander across the ceiling. With increasing age the leaves grow larger on plants in the ground, but I doubt whether this would happen when planted in a pot. *F. pumila* has an even smaller form which is more suited for growing in very small hanging baskets, but this one is not so easy to find.

Also evergreen and sturdy, although not clingers, are the cotoneasters and pyracanthas. There are several varieties of *Cotoneaster horizontalis* (which can also be deciduous and semi-deciduous in cooler climates) and all are good. The rigid branches will need some support, but not a great deal, and they will create lovely patterns against a light wall. The added bonus of clusters of small white flowers and bright red berries make them very valuable for cold or temperate climates, especially in winter. Pyracanthas produce even bigger and better clusters of berries, but those I have seen have all been very thorny, which is not a good attribute for balcony culture. As there are many forms, it could be worth looking around for a thornless, or not-too-thorny one, if you

My robust stephanotis was only about three years old when this picture was taken. The vine will grow in temperate as well as many tropical areas. Stephanotis has been beloved as a wedding flower for many generations.

have a corner where it could stay in the background.

The matter of thorns must also be watched if you think about planting the lovely night-flowering cereus. Here too, there are a number of varieties, some quite thornless. The one I have, which grows equally well in the temperate climates of Sydney or southern California as it does in Hawaii, is quite thornless, yet many of those rambling over walls and hillsides around Honolulu are very prickly indeed. Actually, although the flowers of the latter are very beautiful and much lauded, those on the thornless variety (known variously as 'Belle de Nuit' or 'Princess of the night', *Selenicereus nocturnus* seems to me to be better, and have the same beautiful, but very strong fragrance. *Selenicereus nocturnus* is sometimes mistaken for *Epiphyllum oxypetalum*.

Cereus will grow from just a short section of stem, prefers rich soil and will thrive in either full sun or semi-shade. They can stand fairly low night temperatures, down to about 4-5°C. As the leaves and stems are quite heavy and fleshy a fairly heavy pot will be needed. The stems will not need much support if grown against a wall or screen as they are quite strong. I have one about a metre tall which is self-supporting. They will, of course, grow much taller if allowed enough space, but would need a larger pot.

There are other cereus which flower in the daytime, all with very beautiful flowers. I have only grown the night-flowering one, and so am not sure about the suitability of the others to pot culture.

Don't overlook the annual climbers, even though their life span is shorter than those already listed. They can give very decorative results. Most beloved of these would be the sweet peas, and whilst one can hardly hope for the very tall growth of plants in the ground, a reasonably deep trough and the best of soil will produce acceptable results. Some kind of wire or string frame is needed, of course, for tendrils to cling to. It could be worth trying to find the perennial variety. The great plus with annual sweet peas is that winter-flowering as well as spring-and summer-flowering varieties can be had. Seed should be soaked in warm water for a day or two before sowing about 1-2 cm deep. Give fertiliser every month.

The gay nasturtiums can be used for quick results; not much coddling is needed for these! Also if you like orange shades, the bright little *Thunbergia alata* (black-eyed Susan) grows well in containers. It can often be found in nursery pots already in bloom. It will quickly climb on a trellis or frame to give a long-flowering bright background. Another 'quickie' is *Cobea scandens* (cup-and-saucer vine) with its fascinating flowers which change from green to purple with many shades in between. Stems are quite long too, making them excellent for cutting, if you can bear to cut your balcony flowers. *Cobea* likes a sunny position. Unfortunately, it is not possible to move climbing plants about to keep up with the sun's movements as you can with compact plants. Perhaps if you know which way those precious rays are heading you could train the long growth in that direction. Often the plants will do this for themselves.

Two annual climbers which I have grown in several different climates with equal success are morning glory, (*Ipomoea* 'Heavenly Blue') and its night-blooming cousin, the moonflower, which is white. Both grow incredibly fast. I once measured the morning glory's daily rate of growth, and found it to be about 20 cm a day! Of course, this was in Hawaii's tropical climate, where this rapid growth rate unfortunately also means a far shorter life-span than is the case in cooler climates. Even its brief glory is something to cherish, if only for being able to get close (as one *can* on a balcony) to that miraculous colour so aptly named 'Heavenly Blue'. In temperate and cool climates, this can be enjoyed for many more weeks. It can be worthwhile, if you start one right at the beginning of spring, to plant a succession of seeds, say each month right up till autumn. These seeds also will succeed better if soaked first. They won't need as long as those of the sweet peas, 24 hours should do, and soil need not be as rich. Nip dead blooms off each day or so to prolong flowering.

Although it lacks the breathtaking blue shade, moonflower is just as exciting in a quite different way. There is still the rapid growth, but the joy of these white flowers comes in the evening, when one can watch the slow unfolding of the umbrella-like buds from the neatly furled stage to the final glory of the beautiful round flower. In some areas there will be a quite distinct perfume, which seems to belong to only this member of the big group of convolvulaceous plants but this is not always present. There are other colours and varieties available in this family of annual climbers, but none, to me, equal these two. *Ipomoea* 'Heavenly Blue' and moonflower can be grown in the same pot as they require very little root room. This will give you a 'day-and-night' effect. For a quite short time in early morning they'll be in flower together, but only until moonflower goes to bed for the day.

16

Plants for hanging baskets

Whether or not you will be able to grow hanging basket plants successfully on your balcony will be largely determined by the amount of wind to which it is subjected. This will also govern the types of plants you can grow. Some of the hardier ones will survive even when being spun around and around for much of the day. I have seen coleuses grow successfully under these conditions. They are extremely hardy, grow quickly from cuttings, and if you can get an assortment of colours and leaf forms, they will be decorative for many weeks. Good watering is essential, as it is for all basket-grown plants.

When you start your basket, put one of the several kinds of water-retaining plastic foam preparations in with the potting soil. If your garden shop does not have any of these, go to a supermarket and get a packet of the plastic foam filling that is sold for stuffing cushions. This will serve admirably. It will greatly help to keep the roots damp. In hot weather you will still need to water quite often. There are some useful plastic waterers with long curved spouts which save one from the business of having to climb up on chairs if the plants are very high. Also some of the spray atomisers available are fitted with

such long nozzles. Look around for these handy items in garden stores and supermarkets.

Geraniums, accustomed to growing in windy window-boxes for centuries, will not complain about hanging basket conditions, but they do ask for some sun. There are many kinds to choose from; compact growers and the trailing varieties are available. If you do have a sunny location, think also of petunias which can be very colourful. There are many new varieties. The cascade types, which will give gay colour and perfume for many weeks in summer are especially suitable for baskets. Beautiful effects can be created using either all one colour, an assortment, or just red and white. Also you can achieve lovely effects by combining petunias with other flowers such as pansies, violas, ageratum, lobelia, marigolds, geraniums, and so on.

Sometimes several types of flowers can be combined to make a 'ball' effect by using wire baskets lined with sphagnum moss (sometimes called 'florists' moss') and then inserting the plants between the wires at the sides of the baskets as well as planting them on the top. The moss lining must be about 3 cm thick to retain both

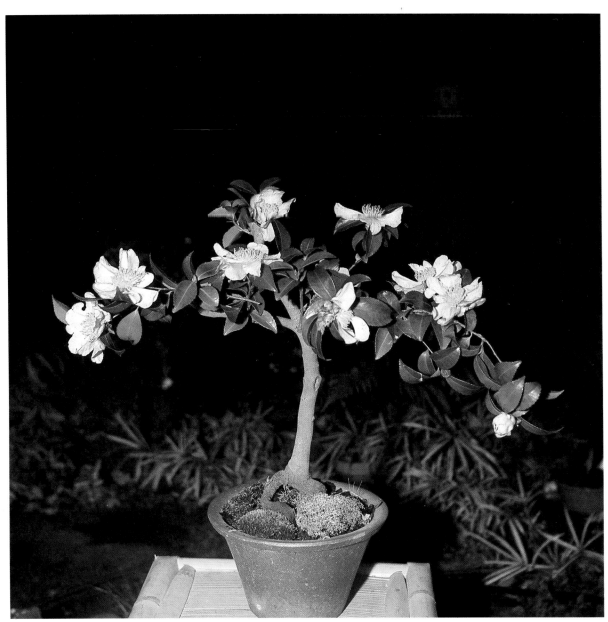

Camellia sasanqua 'Pink Pearl' grown as a bonsai. Although the flowers of this variety are short-lived the foliage is decorative enough to justify a year-round place on a balcony. It has the advantage of flowering ahead of the japonica types.

This camellia ('Dixie Knight') looks attractive against this brick wall.

The beautiful roots of the Chinese banyan are a feature of this 'root-over-rock' style bonsai. The banyans, members of the large *Ficus* genus, adapt to a wide variety of climates, and also grow well indoors.

Bougainvillea 'Mary Palmer' with its two-toned flowers is so versatile that it can grow into a tall tree, or be tamed into a wonderful bonsai. This was shown, with well-earned acclaim, at a Honolulu bonsai display. A good deal of patience and know-how is needed for this effect, but it can be interesting to try to emulate it.

The lovely cyclamen are for the cool climate gardeners. They like cold nights, and a couple of hours of morning sun and a sheltered position to protect the lovely flowers from wind. They have the advantage of being able to be brought indoors if weather is unkind. There they will be happy on a window sill which has the necessary morning sun. They can be grown from bulbs or seed.

Mauve azalea 'Margaret Davis' and its darker relative are both Satsuki types. Hardy, easily shaped, and late-flowering, this variety is ideal for bonsai training into any shape.

Ingenious use has been made of an antique Roman wine jar in this glass-enclosed area.

moisture and soil, and it also should be about 3 cm higher than the soil on the top.

The soil used must be as lightweight as possible, because these baskets, being necessarily large, will be quite heavy when wet. You need a basket at least 30 cm and preferably 35 cm in diameter. Heavy feeding is essential also as much space is occupied by the moss which does not provide nourishment. A good general fertiliser should be given every two weeks, or alternatively add liquid fertiliser to water each day.

You can make smaller ball, or sphere-type baskets by using a smaller basket and following the same procedure with smaller plants such as alyssum, lobelia or violas. I once saw a beautiful effect on a patio where these hanging 'balls' consisted of alternating white and purple alyssum, and edging the patio beneath them were matching pots of the same alternating colours. Of course you can use ivy or any of the hardier evergreens in the same way. These would last longer than the annual flowers which also need more attention in the matter of removing the spent flowers.

Generally speaking, plastic baskets with clip-on saucers are much easier to use than the wire ones, although they will not, of course, do for the special effects just described. They are easier to position than the wire ones, which lack anything to catch drips, unless of course you are able to hang them above a good-sized plant which can take care of the surplus water. These and wire baskets both come in the half-round shapes which are so good for hanging flat on a wall.

For the shaded balconies where wind is not too great a problem, nothing is lovelier for baskets than the gracefully drooping fuchsias. There are so many varieties that I will not attempt to enumerate them here. Some are more pendulous than others, and most garden shops will carry stocks of all types. If you buy those already planted in baskets you can be sure of their suitability, but any of those with soft, pendulous-looking stems will be fine.

The Wandering Jew seen hanging on the right of this photograph is actually growing in a teapot. The hardy stems cascade both from the top of the pot and the spout. This is certainly an unusual and successful hanging 'basket'.

Fuchsias are lovely in half-baskets against the wall too. If you know of a good potter, it could be worth while getting some half-round planters, into which pots could be fitted, made. Sometimes these can be found in garden shops, and if you can find one of the type copied from the classical Italian designs these can be very decorative, especially when filled with ivy as they often are in Italian gardens.

Primulas and cinerarias make attractive basket plants for shaded balconies, as do the many colours of impatiens (busy Lizzie), that hardy little warrior now being produced in attractive variegated forms. The trailing campanulas are lovely too, and have the advantage of being perennial, as do the hardier types of fern and the old reliable wandering Jew (or weary Willie) in variegated forms. The donkey's tail sedum, with its long, rope-like 'tails' often growing up to 1 metre in length, is very decorative and hardy, tolerating either shade or almost full sun in most areas. There is also a small-leaved plant that I really love, and this is *Ceropegia woodii* (or hearts entwined, to give it its more romantic popular name, derived from its prettily speckled heart-shaped leaves). The flowers are not exciting, but the long pendulous stems with all their little hearts are very appealing. This plant prefers shade but it will take some sun also.

Another flowering plant which also likes shade is *Zygocactus truncatus,* or Christmas cactus, which can be found in many attractive colours now. It must be kept quite moist except during its resting period just after flowering, when watering should be reduced. Also give less water when buds are forming, as overwatering at this time could cause them to drop. This plant needs a fairly coarse compost or leaf mould.

No list of hanging basket suggestions should conclude without mention of the lovely *Schizanthus* (poor man's orchid). Beautiful either in pots or baskets, the masses of tiny orchid-like flowers come in a lovely range of colours. This is an annual which needs a protected location because of its brittle leaves and stems. For partly enclosed balconies it is ideal and can be grown in many climates. It can be raised from seed, sown uncovered in a dark cool place. If this is a problem, it may be possible to get seedlings or small potted plants. It is worth searching for.

The different Hedera in this hanging terracota container will grow well on windy balconies.

Many of the vines suggested in chapter 15 on climbing plants will grow well in baskets. Some of the fast-growing ones will need to be pruned, or to have their long stems looped back into the basket. This is a good way of thickening your planting, as many of these vines, such as the hoyas, ceropegias and philodendrons have aerial roots which will provide new plants when tucked back into the soil. These can be removed later if you want to start additional plants.

Where there is enough sun, bougainvilleas will make excellent hanging basket plants. Be sure to get the softer-stemmed varieties. They will take a good deal of wind, and will also do well if the baskets are hung from a trellis on a sunny wall. Even if you do not have half-baskets, it is a simple matter to adjust the wires of the round plastic baskets so as to let them hang against a wall.

Smaller plants such as lobelia and the cascade form of petunias can also be used in pots suspended in wire rings which can also be hooked into a trellis. A trough filled with plants just beneath this trellis will take care of the drips in these cases. If you are not able to find a trough with a matching tray, get one made by the nearest sheet-metal worker, but be sure it is galvanised.

This luxurious *Nephrolepsis exaltata elegantissima* completely disguises the basket in which it is planted.

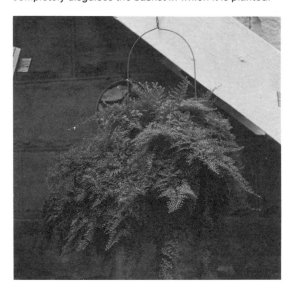

17

Bonsai for balconies & terraces

Bonsai can be grown quite successfully on balconies, even those exposed to a good deal of wind, if the right varieties are chosen. In fact, some of the pines, especially those most prized in the Japanese connoisseurs' collections, have come from the high mountains where the strong winds were originally responsible for their wonderful, gnarled shapes.

No amount of careful wiring in nurseries can ever equal the shapes thus created. That is why the more treasured and certainly the most expensive of these marvellous little trees are those originally carefully dug up in the high mountains, their long long roots being painstakingly wrapped and then planted in the ground in the specialist nurseries for a period of years during which these roots are periodically shortened back, a little at a time, until they are finally able to be potted in the incredibly small, shallow containers, in which they are finally sold, and in which, if they fall into the right hands, they will continue to live for many years, probably centuries. Most of the pines in this category are the Japanese black pine *(Pinus thunbergii),* red pine *(P. densiflora)* and five-needled pine *(P. pentaphylla).*

There are also several varieties of juniper which are used in the same way.

Most of us must be content to buy our pines or junipers from a Western nursery where they are now becoming more readily available, either already trained, or in the form of young seedlings. The red and black pines will grow quite quickly. The five-needle type is much slower, and seedlings take many years to reach a reasonable size. Space will not permit here a detailed description of the cultivation of these pines and junipers, but there are now many excellent books on the subject of bonsai, perhaps the most authoritative being *Miniature Trees and Landscapes* by Yuji Yoshimura and Giovanna Halford. I was lucky enough to attend a course of lessons at the former's Kofu-en nursery in Tokyo many years ago, and it was in this nursery that I saw an idea that could be used with advantage on windy balconies to prevent the plants being blown over in a strong wind. This was to pass wire at each end of the rectangular pots, right over the soil and then to secure these wires to the shelf on which the plants stood. This was used in the case of a number of plants which were mounted upon platforms set on top of posts dotted about the nursery; presumably to display to better advantage the choicest specimens.

When growing bonsai, make a point of collecting a number of heavy decorative waterworn or weathered stones. These will not only add greatly to the decorative effect of your plants, but will also serve the useful purposes of helping to anchor them against strong winds and conserving moisture, especially in the case of the very shallow containers so frequently used which dry out so quickly. There are, of course, a great many ways of combining the stones as part of the actual planting, by setting the plants on top of them, or in any small hollows, with the roots going down the sides into the soil beneath. This is particularly effective with the small figs (*Ficus* spp.) which have such ornamental roots, often as important as the branches and the foliage. The pines already mentioned also lend themselves to this type of planting. They acquire a look of greater age when the roots are thus seen on the surface. You must follow instructions in doing these plantings, so that there are enough roots in the soil to maintain a healthy plant and, most important, great care must be taken in keeping these plants well watered so that these exposed roots will not dry out too much.

Other plants which will stand up to quite a lot of wind are the pyracanthas (formerly classified as *Crataegus)* and the smaller forms of cotoneaster, all of which have beautiful berries, are fast-growing, and respond very well to shaping. Then there are the flowering cherries and the *Prunus* genus so beloved of the Japanese, and the beautiful little crab-apples, and so many other fruiting trees, including the big citrus family, with its beautiful small forms; the charming little Calomondin orange, the Chinoti, the various cumquats, and even the normal Valencia orange and lemons can be dwarfed if grafted on to small-growing stocks. And pears, quinces, pomegranates. The list is long, but the choice can be agonising when space is limited!

So, one solution is to set about seeing how many can be accommodated in the space available. If there is a good area of wall, try a sort of 'bookshelf' arrangement, with the lower shelves wider than the higher ones so that the shelves above (if made of wood) will not keep too much light away from the bottom row of plants. If the shelves are made of glass, this problem will not arise, assuming that the plants are staggered in such a way that none is directly above another. Fortunately, there are many types of stands to be had these days. If you are fortunate enough to have a post on your balcony, you could put a series of rounded shelves around it. Some furniture stores stock wrought-iron 'baker's racks', with a series of shelves which would accommodate a good number of plants.

It is a good idea to concentrate on keeping the plants small in order to have more variety. The big spreading types are best for open gardens where they can be seen to better advantage anyway. We who have only a little area must 'scale down'. All of the varieties already enumerated with the exception of the banyans must have a sunny aspect.

This applies to most flowering and fruiting trees, but it is especially so for most 'needled' evergreens. If deprived of sun the shoots will tend to grow out weak and 'leggy', which of course will not contribute to the sturdy, compact form which is an essential of all bonsai.

There are many varieties however, which will thrive in partial, or even complete, shade. These include the many varieties of the lovely maples, azaleas and miniature rhododendrons, the cycads, bamboos, and, perhaps the most adaptable of all, the several smaller forms of the large *Ficus* genus. One need not even specify 'smaller forms' I realise, looking across the room to my little 30-cm-high specimen of the same member of this genus whose full-grown brothers are so huge as to be among the 'sights' in several of the Hawaiian Islands and in many other tropical regions; magnificent giants which cover enormous areas of ground, sending down aerial roots which, when they reach the ground, become trees themselves, so that in a few years there is a large grove, all attached to the original parent tree. The wonderful gnarled trunks of these trees are reproduced in miniature in the bonsai forms, and as this takes place at a relatively early age, one certainly does not have to wait years and years to grow a quite ancient-looking specimen of this Bengal banyan *(Ficus benghalensis)*.

In the warmer climates it is not difficult to buy small plants of this ficus in 100-mm pots which will already have begun to show signs of a fairly heavy trunk. A similar fig which I grew in Sydney, *F. rubiginosa,* had the same characteristics, and even a six or seven year-old seedling would already have quite a bulbous trunk. It seems that the latter variety grows better in cooler districts than does *F. benghalensis.* With both of these, it is best to push them along fairly quickly in not-too-small pots for the first few years so that they make good branch and leaf growth which can be pruned often to create a bushy top. They are both extremely hardy, growing either in sun, semi-shade or even complete shade. This gives them the very valuable advantage of being suitable for year-round indoor culture, something to which only a few other bonsai will submit.

Most of the other species of the *Ficus* genus have this endearing trait, and one which is also ideal for bonsai in the charming little cherry banyan, or mistletoe banyan *(Ficus diversifolia).* A much slower grower, this little tree is covered, even from infancy, in attractive little green, whitish, and sometimes reddish berries. It has small rounded leaves, grows easily from cuttings and lends itself to a variety of shapes.

Returning to the larger, fast-growing varieties, we have a treasure in the graceful, pendulous weeping fig or benjamin banyan *(Ficus benjamina)* which, like its cousin from Bengal, grows into a very large spreading tree, but can also be tamed into a most attractive indoor or balcony specimen. It is extremely hardy, very decorative, and adapts perfectly to being kept indoors for apparently unlimited periods, provided that its small requirements of reasonable amounts of light, air and water are met.

F. benjamina's graceful pendulous habit of growth makes it suitable for many more purposes than was the case with its heavier-leaved cousins, *F. decora* and *F. elastica.* Rate of growth depends entirely on climate. In Hawaii, it reaches 2 metres in just a few years, but in colder climates grows more slowly and is correspondingly more expensive. Whether large or small, it is a treasure. If grown outdoors, it will take sun, but it appears to be happier in shade or semi-shade. This tree has now become as fashionable as was *F. decora* a few years ago, and is consequently not always easy to get. It is worthwhile looking around for small potted seedlings, or trying some cuttings if you have a friend with a large tree. It would have to be treated as one of your larger bonsai, because of its open habit of growth, but I believe it could be kept at around 45 cm high for quite a time.

Among the flowering plants suitable for bonsai possibly the first choices would be bougainvilleas for hot climates and azaleas for cooler regions. Japanese nurserymen have had wonderful results with their Satsuki azaleas. The small-growing Gumpo types now becoming more available are ideal for this purpose where space is limited. In some areas they will have a fairly long flowering period, but it must be remembered that few azaleas are particularly interesting when not in flower, unless, of course, they are ancient bonsai, whose branch formation is beautiful in itself.

There are many lovely varieties of *Prunus* spp., cherry and other deciduous trees to which this will also apply, and, if space is very limited, it might be best to pass these up in favour of the evergreens, or plants such as the lovely *Pieris japonica* (formerly *Andromeda)* with its lovely lily-of-the-valley-like racemes of white or pink bells which stay in bloom for such a long time. The leaves of this plant remain on throughout the year, but the new spring growth is a beautiful pink; it is so decorative, in fact that many Japanese gardens feature the leaves rather than the flowers. This lovely plant is only for the cold, or cooler climates, however.

Choice of suitable plants will therefore depend entirely on your climate (see chapter 1). A careful look around the local nurseries will not only give an idea of what subjects do well in your area, but may also reveal some items suitable for cutting down into bonsai. When the bonsai bug first bit me, I used to haunt the older nurseries, and sometimes the smaller one-man kind, where neglected plants had been thrust into the background, having not been regarded as good enough for seasonal re-potting. These areas could be positive goldmines, and often went at bargain prices. You will enjoy the challenge of finding well-advanced trees (usually in too-big old tins) taking them home, and pruning back roots and branches. The final result may take a few seasons to achieve perfection in some cases, in many others near-perfection is assured as soon as the pruning process is completed.

This is the perfect solution for the older gardener who is not willing to wait for the maturing of seedlings and cuttings, and certainly this 'instant bonsai' method can be enormously rewarding. One must be prepared to search diligently however, for competition is great these days with so many bonsai addicts always on the prowl. Even when fairly large branches have to be cut back, it is possible to disguise these cuts by carefully filing down the stubs. After a time they will blend into the colour of the rest of the trunk. It may be

advisable to do the root pruning in instalments at one-year intervals. Remember that when you prune roots you must cut off a corresponding amount of the top growth.

It is a pity that many older gardeners are put off attempting to grow bonsai by the constant emphasis on age so often seen at shows and in literature on the subject. The first question the average person asks on seeing one of these trees is, 'How old is it?' So that it is hardly surprising that some nurseries tend to exaggerate age to meet this too-oft-repeated query. After all, what does it matter, if the little tree is a beautiful object?

There are some plants that can be grown from cuttings quickly, and which will manage to look reasonably mature in a very few years. Outstanding among these is the willow. Any of the several varieties are suitable. If a thick branch is cut in late winter or early spring, left in water till a good root system is formed, then potted in an attractive Chinese or Japanese pot, you will soon have the interesting task of cutting and shaping branches to make a compact form before allowing them to hang in their inimitably graceful way when the plant is placed on a high stand or shelf. Do not be disappointed if your cuttings die when first potted. They sometimes do, so have several on hand at once. You can always give the surplus away. Once they are established, growth will be so rapid (if you have the right conditions) that both roots and top growth will need pruning twice a year. At least a third of the roots can be safely cut away. Replant in good rich soil. For more information see my book, *Gardening in Pots*. Willows like plenty of water, and the pots can even stand in saucers of water.

Quick results can also be had from fast-growing seedlings. Possibly the most satisfactory of these are the lovely Japanese maples. Large trees nearly always have a crop of seedlings beneath them, and these, when lifted and potted in good soil will grow very rapidly and are very amenable to shaping. In areas where growth is rapid, some wiring of the trunks will be needed but the wire must not be left on too long. Check it frequently lest it cut into the bark. Scars left this way will never grow out. If necessary, loosen the wires every few months. You can make a small group planting of these little maples in a wide shallow container. They look very effective grouped towards one end of rectangular Japanese bonsai pots. There is often a problem in getting the right size saucers for these pots, but either a small tray, or those shallow plastic or styrofoam trays on which fruit, vegetables and cuts of meat are sold in the supermarkets serve very well. They are surprisingly strong, especially if painted top and bottom. Black looks best, shows fewer marks and fits in with the Japanese theme.

Pine seedlings are well worth trying if you happen to be in an area where they grow well (usually cold or moderately cool regions). Sometimes these can be difficult to lift, as they put down long tap roots, and it could be just as simple to raise them from seed. When we lived in the cold mountains, I used to pick up cones which had fallen from the varieties of pine that I liked best, waiting till they had just begun to open. The seeds fall out easily if you knock the cones together. They will usually come up quite quickly; some types take longer, but wait for them.

Plant the seeds in soil containing at least some portion of soil from where the parent tree is growing as this will contain a useful fungus called mycorrhiza which has a beneficial effect on the roots of pines. When the time comes to re-pot any of your pines, remember again to get some soil from beneath healthy pines, even if it needs to be combined with a richer sandy mix sold especially for bonsai. When the time comes to pot these little pines on, it is also best to shorten the long tap root that the seedlings will have made, otherwise it will go round and around their next pot. Also they should be encouraged to form side roots. Take off about one third. Some

varieties of pine will, like the *Ficus,* form quite thick trunks at an early age, making them perfect for bonsai.

Remember that pines will not be happy indoors. If you want to take your pet bonsai into the house for a time, do not keep it there too long. Give it a sunny position.

Holly is another freely-seeding plant which makes very attractive bonsai with, or without, its lovely berries. A search beneath mature bushes will nearly always turn up good little seedlings, the older ones possibly already well on the way to having a good branching form. Thinking of holly reminds me of another lovely plant with leaves very like a miniature variegated holly, but with wonderfully fragrant flowers. This is *Osmanthus aquifolium,* which is easily trained into lovely forms. Its relative, *Osmanthus fragrans,* has the most beautifully apricot-scented flowers. They are quite insignificant, but will scent the air all around. I have grown it as a bonsai, but it is not so adaptable as *O. aquifolium,* as its leaves and stems are very stiff. It grows readily from cuttings in cooler climates, and this gives you a good chance of shaping the little plants from infancy. It is much faster-growing than *O. aquifolium,* but they are both treasures, and not nearly as well known in some regions as they deserve to be. *O. fragrans* is seen quite often in Japanese gardens.

Another plant that few people would think of growing as a bonsai but which can be most satisfactory is rosemary. Either the upright or the prostrate form will train remarkably well. Being fairly fast-growing, frequent clipping is needed, and the clippings are great for cooking. Rosemary is marvellous with roast veal; and of course in soups, stews, casseroles, and finely-chopped in toasted sandwiches. In fact, when you discover how useful this plant is, you will probably need at least two plants.

There are actually more plants suitable for bonsai available to cold-climate gardeners than in the tropical areas. This is good, because in the long winters when there are few flowers and many trees are bare, a collection of bonsai can provide a great amount of interest and decoration. Even in cases of deciduous varieties their shapes are attractive all the year round. Camellias, of course, really come into their own in winter, and many varieties are suitable for bonsai. Oddly enough the best I have seen were *C. sasanqua* types, and although I have stated in chapter 13 on camellias that I do not recommend the sasanquas for larger balcony plants, but well pruned in bonsai the prostrate form can be very attractive. There are several smaller types also, and they have the added bonus of having glossy evergreen leaves which are always decorative.

Of course, anyone who grows bonsai will sooner or later (and often quite frequently) encounter friends who will shudder at the 'cruelties' inflicted on these 'Poor little tortured trees!' Often the shudderer is one who regularly prunes his hedges and trees and mows his lawns without any thought of being cruel. It is useless to point out that besides the fact that one could hardly accommodate a 15-m pine or maple on one's balcony, these trees are neither dwarfed, starved or stunted. Through careful root and branch pruning and pinching, they are controlled, but not thwarted. The accusation that their small size is the result of neglect and starvation is the direct opposite of the truth. They must have meticulous, regular and, above all, loving care to survive.

As one grower put it. 'You certainly get more mileage as a conversation-promoter, out of one bonsai than you would from three dozen ordinary pot plants. I recommend it to anyone who wants an easy way to get an animated argument going!' The same writer said of her first experience of root-pruning, 'I found the whole operation nerve-racking, rather like cutting your first baby's fingernails for the first time. You know it has to be done, but wonder

how you're going to feel if . . .' I think we must have all had the same misgivings, but one grows bolder with practice and in no time at all we are snipping and shearing away with sometimes too much gusto.

Then it must be remembered that no more than one third of a plant's roots should be removed at one time. Also remember that frequency of root pruning varies with different trees. For instance members of the pine family (and most needled trees) should only be root-pruned every 3 to 5 years, whereas those tough characters, the willows and the wisterias, will probably need it every 6 months in areas where they grow rapidly. It is difficult to lay down definite rules in the light of the great many varieties of plants now being grown as bonsai, and also in the greatly varying conditions in different climates, and even the different conditions in any one country. As I write about willows and wisteria at this moment, I am reminded of how I used to do this twice-yearly root-pruning in Sydney, yet in Hawaii we cannot even grow wisteria at all, and the one tiny piece of willow that I coaxed to root 2 years ago still struggles to live and has grown a bare 4 inches in all that time!

Get a good book on bonsai, for there is much to be learned about this fascinating art. But keep in mind that the best books will probably be written in Japan and will almost certainly deal with conditions in that country (possibly even just one area of it). You will be well advised to more or less 'play it by ear' if yours is a quiet different climate. As with any form of gardening, only careful study of one's own conditions and knowledge gained by experience will ensure any degree of success. But whilst you are gaining this invaluable 'know-how' you will be experiencing the most rewarding (even if often frustrating) of all the pastimes that anyone could hope to enjoy.

Azalea 'Phoebus' has been a favourite for many years and is still well worth growing. Well suited to container culture, and long flowering, it is a lovely glowing red.

This colourful petunia border edges the balcony of an apartment. They have a gaiety that is unmatched by many annuals and are almost as universally popular as geraniums. (Photograph by Stirling Macoboy.)

Poinsettia, the 'flower of Christmas', usually seen in its red form is worth seeking out in yellow and pink. These softer colours are useful for teaming with other light shades when reds can sometimes be too dominant.

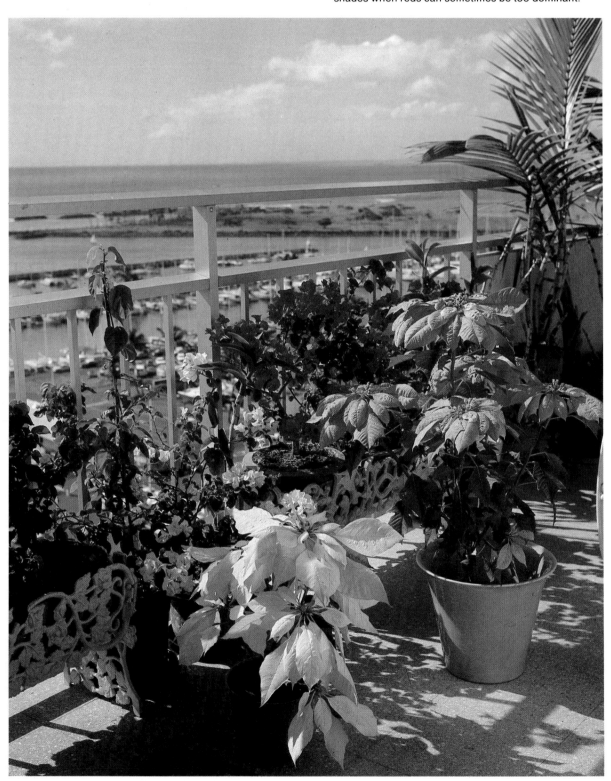

18

Vegetables in containers

The staggering rise in food prices all over the world has brought about a tremendous interest in vegetable growing in the past few years, and even apartment dwellers are experimenting with the smaller-growing items, often with surprising success. I am one of these experimenters, and I would strongly recommend this most interesting and rewarding form of balcony gardening to anyone with even just a few feet of available space.

There is just one 'must', however, and this is sunshine. Even a few hours of sun will suffice, preferably morning sun, but this is not essential. Midday or afternoon will be better than none, especially if reflected heat can be given from warm walls. It will help too, to place pots close to a wall if possible in order to have as much protection against wind, which presents the biggest problem to most balcony gardeners.

Sometimes a glass, perspex or wire mesh shelter can be erected to help break the main force of destructive winds. This need not be high enough to cause concern as to the regulations governing most apartment or unit buildings; sometimes a fly-screen door laid on its side against the balcony railing will break the main force without excluding too much of the all-important sun.

If you are at ground-level this problem will not be nearly so acute. You might even be able to try a charming idea which I saw recently, of having a screen of climbing beans! The variety used was 'Scarlet Runner' which have the extra bonus of red flowers. The beans were planted in long troughs from which heavy string was stretched to the board which edged the balcony ceiling above. The same idea could be used against a wall, if there was a danger of the 'bean screen' excluding too much light from the rest of the balcony. This could be easily controlled by the spacing of the beans at planting time. In either case, there would be room for other low-growing items in front of the beans. Lettuces would be good here as they, like beans, give quick results.

If this arrangement would not fit in with the existing scheme, or if there is not a suitable board to which to nail the strings, it could be worth while trying the beans in big round or square pots with a tall wire-netting cylinder in the centre, or a tripod made from stakes. Bush or dwarf beans will also do quite well. Pots could be mounted on casters so that they can be moved to catch the most sun. Many stores now sell various sized wood platforms fitted with casters for easy removal of plants, or it could be cheaper to make such platforms at home. They are handy for moving house plants as well.

For smaller-sized pots, which can still be quite heavy to lift if soil is on the heavy side, use a mixture containing a good proportion of vermiculite, which is feather light but still very good for retention of moisture and also for good drainage. Many ready-to-use potting mixtures contain a good deal of this medium. These pot plant mixtures, although more expensive than ordinary garden soil, are usually worth the extra cost. They are easy to handle and the good brands will have well-balanced proportions, and will be sterilised. Most have some fertiliser added, but this will need to be supplemented in most cases when the vegetables get under way. I still believe the best fertiliser to be animal manure, even though this may present some problems in confined areas, but poultry manure can usually be bought in quite small packages. It must be used sparingly if plants and pots are small. Failing this, any general garden fertiliser can be used, with perhaps the addition of some liquid fertiliser when plants come into flower. A number of people prefer to grow their vegetables in troughs and tubs even though they have garden space. They maintain that care is much easier when plants are in containers; certainly one does not have to stoop so far, and weeding is far easier. Also I know people who have grown tomatoes by both methods, and assert that those in containers are superior and less trouble. One man in California has a small area in his garden where he grows all his vegetables in a series of redwood troughs arranged very interestingly in a series of built-up tiers. These redwood troughs can be made by a handyman, and even if you do not plan on such a large-scale arrangement as this, if you live in a terrace house one or two would make a decorative edging for a terrace, or on either side of a path. Discarded round washing-machine bowls and half casks can be used very effectively also.

The balcony gardener has usually to be content with smaller containers, for, even where space may permit, there is always the difficult problem of finding a drip tray to catch water drainage. Troughs present a problem in such cases, unless one is lucky enough to have a balcony with a drainage gutter. On the whole it is usually simpler to have a series of large plastic pots, with either plastic or metal saucers beneath. For the larger size, where saucers are hard to find, inexpensive metal or plastic drink trays will serve very well. If there is a sunny wall which could carry a section of trellis, some climbing plants could still be planted in these pots at its base.

The number of vegetables suitable for container growing is quite large. I have even seen corn growing in the large tubs, but a good deal of space is needed for this. Probably the ideal plant for container growing is the tomato in its various forms. Whilst the large-fruiting kinds can be used, generally speaking the smaller types are easier to manage and give a very good yield. I have found that the very small 'cherry' tomato, also known as 'Tiny Tim', does extremely well, and produces clusters of fruit very early in its life.

Also small, though larger than the cherry-sized one, with fruit about 2-3 cm wide is 'Small Fry' which produces its fruit also in clusters of 6 to 10. Slightly larger again are 'Pixie' and 'Patio Hybrid' with fruit 3-5 cm in diameter, also borne in clusters. 'Pixie' grows about 45 cm high and 'Patio Hybrid' and 'Small Fry' somewhat taller. 'Tiny Tim' averages about 30 cm. The last, being the smallest, can be grown in a 15-cm pot, but the others will do best in a 30-cm container. Support will be needed in all cases, and this can take the form of one or more stakes or a cylinder of chicken wire surrounding each plant. A small trellis can be used and 'Small Fry' will grow quite decoratively in hanging baskets. Actually, these small tomatoes can be grown on a sunny windowsill, but they must be assured of good light and plenty of sun. Sown in autumn, they will produce throughout the winter in temperate climates, especially if the room in which they are grown is centrally heated.

It must always be remembered that vegetables grown in containers will require watering even more regularly than those in the ground. Unless the weather is cloudy or wet, they will almost certainly need water every day. Feeding must be attended to at regular intervals also, using either a general fertiliser or in the case of tomatoes one of the special types of tomato food. Quantities shown on the package should be halved for any plants grown in pots.

Trouble from pests or disease will vary with climate and season. There are special tomato and vegetable dusts. If you find it necessary to use a general insecticide, take care that you do not use any of the poisonous sprays too close to harvesting time. Usually those containing pyrethrum are safest for vegetable crops. Also see chapter 20 on pests.

As to which vegetables to grow, the variety is enormous. If your plot is very small it would be worth searching for some of the 'mini' type vegetables, now being sold for smaller areas. These are small

It seems hard to believe that this is a corner of a garden on the sixteenth floor of a New York apartment building. Mr Stewart Mott has erected a fence to give protection from wind, and an assortment of vegetables grows beneath the weigelia and fruiting trees.

replicas of normal varieties especially hybridised for present-day requirements. If not available, it could be worth while to send for some mail-order seed catalogues. Do not mistake small-fruiting varieties which grow on normal-sized plants for these miniatures. The latter are true midgets, both fruit and plants.

19

Herbs

It should be no problem to grow all the herbs you will require on your balcony. Most of them can be kept small enough to fit around the edges of larger tubs or pots, and an edging of parsley, chives or basil will look quite attractive and save space.

Basil can be useful, as it is the tallest of these, to plant beneath trees that have lost their leaves or become a little 'leggy', and it is an accommodating plant and can easily be kept low if you do not need this type of camouflage. I find it enormously useful for a range of recipes, and always keep a few leaves in the jar of oil and vinegar salad dressing. It gives a very pleasant flavour to this, is good finely chopped in the salad itself, and is especially harmonious with tomatoes. When you have a good crop it can be dried for winter use, as can most herbs. It is very easily raised from seed scattered where it is to grow. This can be done also with parsley. If you have difficulty growing basil from seed it is always possible to find small plants of this ever-popular plant.

Chives are always useful and there are usually several varieties to be had, so why not have an assortment. Do not despair if after a time your chives die away. This is normal and seasonal, and they will probably re-appear next spring.

Oregano is nice and compact for growing with other plants and so are the various kinds of thyme. Mint is best kept in a pot to itself, as you will realise if you've had it romp all over garden beds,

and tried to track the long tenacious roots. Growth will not be so rampant in a pot, naturally, but it is nevertheless inclined to take possession and choke other plants. For this reason it should not be included in any container of mixed herbs.

If you do not have any suitable large containers in which to grow your herbs with larger plants, the best way to plant them is in one of the old-fashioned strawberry pots now back in circulation, and being used for almost everything except strawberries! These tall pots take up the minimum of space, yet accommodate a surprising number of plants. They look very attractive too, especially if you take care to plant them so that the taller ones do not obscure the more compact varieties. These pots must be planted carefully so that the plants do not sink beneath their holes when the soil settles.

Begin by putting a curved piece of crock or broken china over the drainage hole, curved side up, with a layer of gravel or some coarse fibre to ensure the very necessary drainage and prevent soil penetrating down the sides of the crock. Then add just enough soil to reach the base of the lowest row of pockets. Water this soil before planting, and when it has settled plant the herbs from *inside* the pot, pulling the leaves gently to the outside. If planted from the outside, the roots may suffer. Now, cover the roots lightly, but before adding the next layer of soil, put a small piece of shade cloth over the opening of each 'pocket' to prevent the soil running out. Then proceed to fill up to the base of the next pocket, proceeding as before, and letting the soil settle (even pressing it down gently) before planting each row. It could even be left and watered for several days before planting the herb in the top opening.

General purpose plant mix is the best for these plants, with some liquid plant food about once a month. Use the smaller growing herbs such as thyme, marjoram, lemon balm, chervil, oregano, and chives for the side pockets. Parsley is good for the top section as it will not spread too much and keep the sun and light from the lower plants, but chives will serve quite well here also. Dwarf, or prostrate, rosemary would be good to plant in one of the lower pockets, as it can then spread downwards without crowding other plants. You will find it very useful.

The strawberry pot will need to be replanted in a year or so if the herbs have grown strongly. They can then be divided and repotted in new soil.

Borage is an attractive herb, with its pretty blue flowers. Like basil, it is an annual, but easily raised from seed each year. The leaves, with their cucumber-like taste, are a very pleasant addition to fruit cup or punch. The flowers can be effectively crystallised, but they also make a very pretty decoration on sweets, cakes and in drinks when used fresh. Leaves are used in many ways for cooking and chopped in salads. The plant has an ancient reputation for imparting cheerfulness and courage, not to mention a number of healing attributes. It is pretty enough to be grown by itself, but could share a pot or tub with tall plants or trees. Both leaves and flowers of borage can be infused for a herbal tea.

Comfrey, a larger relative of borage has been used since mediaeval times to heal a number of ailments, even having been given the name of 'knit-bone' at one time because of its ability to speed the healing of broken bones. Modern-day health food enthusiasts are very keen on it. If you can find a copy of *Culpeper's Complete Herbal,* written originally in the early seventeenth century and reprinted by W. Foulsham of London, it provides very entertaining reading about this and many other herbs. Its culinary value is not great as the leaves are somewhat tough with prickly hairs and little taste, but much has been said of its curative powers. It can be grown in a large pot, but is a very strong grower, and should not be combined with other plants, as its strong roots (also of great medicinal value) need a pot to themselves. It has been said that comfrey leaves are delicious when dipped in batter and then fried in hot oil.

The way you pick the leaves of your herbs is rather important. Always take first the outside leaves of parsley and chervil. Cut basil sprigs from the top of the plants in order to keep them compact and prevent them from forming flowers and seeds, which will inhibit any further growth. At the end of the season, you can let one basil plant go to seed for next year, but in warm climates they can sometimes

A hanging basket can also be used for growing herbs.

continue for quite a time without dying down if kept cut back. All the varieties of chives are best if continuously kept cut. This helps them to grow better.

A 'must' in even your little garden is a bay tree. These will grow slowly for many years in pots, and are best kept in a pot by themselves. They can be gradually trained into the popular European round or cone shape as you use the aromatic leaves. Here too, the older leaves should be cut first. Although they are sold dried, fresh from the plant they are wonderful for all soups, casseroles and roasts. They are happier in cold than in hot climates, growth being slower in the latter case, but even a small plant will be sufficient for most needs.

It need hardly be emphasised that you must not use pesticides on plants growing in close proximity to herbs. In fact many of the herbs are themselves insect repellents. Basil is credited with not only going well with tomatoes in salads and cooked dishes, but with keeping insects and diseases away from the growing plants. It is also repellent to flies and mosquitoes. Oregano is said to keep beetles away from cucumbers, and tansy is said to discourage ants, aphids and flies. So tansy could be worth trying. Chives planted around roses are supposed to keep aphids away. Rue is said to have great insect-repellent qualities, but as some of the other herbs refuse to grow in close contact with it, it could be best left out of small areas. Dried lavender, rosemary, tansy and lad's love are useful in keeping moths and silverfish away from clothes and books.

Older people have an added reason for growing herbs, however. They are a great help in cooking if you are prescribed a no-salt diet. When my husband's doctor decreed 'No salt, either in cooking or on the table,' it seemed a bleak prospect, but the basil, chives, bay leaves, rosemary and oregano came instantly, and most satisfactorily, to the rescue. We have long since ceased to miss the salt, and everything tastes really better than it did before. With the challenge of getting new flavours into our dishes, I have tried a number of herbs that were formerly only names to me, and I could really recommend this kind of experiment.

Fortunately with the increasing interest in all kinds of herbs throughout the country, garden shops now carry quite good assortments of the better known types, and it would certainly be well worth while to visit a herb farm or specialist nursery to find out which will be best suited to your climate, and to get new varieties to try.

Parsley, mint and thyme grow well together in this plastic tower pot.

20

The inevitable pests

When I first became a balcony gardener, I recall remarking happily that at last I would be able to enjoy my plants and flowers without having to wage constant war against armies of chewing, sucking, crawling and constantly marauding insects that had kept me so busy in my large gardens. 'They'll never come up as high as the fifteenth floor,' I gloated confidently, carefully checking all newly bought plants for any signs of scale, thrip or red spider. Yet within a few weeks great masses of nasty green aphis were pushing and shoving one another for a foothold on every bud and flower of my bougainvilleas, and the horrible little brutes had even burrowed into the centres of the dendrobium orchids right in the living room, whilst red spider mites were spoiling the appearance of many of the leaves. Meanwhile the mealy bugs had come to the party and started in on leaves and stems of the stephanotis, and an ugly brown scale covered the stems and leaves of my lovely jasmine. Yet another variety of scale had started in on the hibiscus, and the busy little ants which had possibly been responsible for spreading so many of these pests were scurrying about like efficient little hosts making sure that everyone got their share of the goodies.

Did you know that little black ants are one of the gardener's greatest trials? They are certainly the hardest to eradicate because of their habit of making nests right down in the bottoms of pots, where it is impossible to reach them, and breeding there in a terribly prolific way. They apparently carry the eggs of aphis and mealy bugs to all parts so that they can feed upon the sticky substance excreted by these insects. They actually 'farm' them, as people farm cows, for their food supply. So first, to get rid of these troublesome little farmers! There are many types of ant poisons to be found, some of which are temporarily effective. Ants can be sprayed with garden insecticides when they can be seen, but unfortunately, most of their feeding and wandering is done at night. It was when we noticed this that we were able to hit upon a weird home remedy that has proved more effective than any of the more sophisticated methods that we have used. This is how it happened. We had been dining one evening on the balcony, and had dropped a papaya (pawpaw) seed. A little later we noticed a huge number of ants crowding to get to this seed, and so it occurred to me that these might make quite a good trap. Accordingly we then spread out some newspaper with a goodly helping of the seeds in the centre and awaited results. Sure enough, in less than half an hour the centre of the paper was black with ants! Here is where speed must be combined with cunning. One must creep up very quietly, and quickly wrap up the paper tightly, wrap it again before enclosing it in a plastic bag and place the parcel in the garbage can. The wrapper-upper needs a partner for this operation, to hold a flashlight, which must be switched on at the last minute, as the ants usually feed in the dark. If you have sugar-eating ants, try mixing some sugar with borax and leave it in little heaps near the nests. This can be an effective poison.

Even though these methods are somewhat laborious, I always prefer any means of insect control to that of using pesticides that could be dangerous to birds and to the appealing little geckos which sometimes run about the walls.

It is perhaps in the field of pest control that the balcony gardener becomes most nostalgic for the garden hose of the down-to-earth days! Oh, for that beautiful strong spray of water which would dislodge aphis and mealy bugs so easily! I find that the latter will sometimes succumb to spraying with a strong spray from an atomiser, and for the more obstinate ones, I keep a second atomiser filled with soapy water. This also kills most types of aphis, but must not be left on the plants longer than 15 or 20 minutes. Follow with a spraying of clear water, as the soap will be too strong for most of the flowers or young leaf shoots to which these pests are attracted.

Some people use detergent for this, and it is easier to use than having to whip up soap, but it may be too strong, especially for more delicate flowers.

This soapy water spray will also control several types of scale but the more stubborn ones should be sprayed with white oil emulsion, of which there are several brands to be had. Be sure to follow the label directions.

For small plants where there are just a few hard-to-reach mealy bugs, many people prefer to use a cotton bud or a small piece of cotton wool wound around a

toothpick or a longer thin stick and dipped in alcohol or methylated spirits. This kills the pest on contact. By the way, if you haven't yet met mealy bugs, they are white and fluffy.

I also use the soapy water treatment for dunking long soft branches of bougainvillea and sprays of orchids which are thickly clustered with aphis. Do this in a wide shallow basin. In this way the pests can be washed out of the deep trumpets in the centres of the orchids and under the curling petals. Leave it on for a short time to catch the stragglers, and then wash off with clear water.

Even if a few escape there will be a fresh population in just a few days because the breeding rate of aphis is phenomenal. The eggs hatch in an incredibly short time. It becomes necessary to make sorties over several days, and then one may hope to have peace for a little while. How lucky are the cold-climate gardeners, whose pests do at least have a dormant period in winter. In a year-round warm climate one has to be eternally vigilant!

There are many other ways of dealing with pests without using dangerous pesticides. English scientist, Mr David Greenstock, has developed a mixture of ground garlic, oil and water which he claims will quickly kill greenfly, caterpillars, wireworms and snails, which plague English gardeners, whilst being harmless to ladybirds, birds and bees, which risk nothing worse than a bad case of halitosis! This is the recipe. Soak 90 g of chopped garlic in 2 teaspoons of kerosene for 24 hours, then add 0.5 L of water and mix well. Add a few mL of an oil-based soap to act as a spreading agent.

Another recipe, which is based on nicotine, should serve as a warning to persistent smokers as to how lethal this habit is! Boil 120 g of non-filter-tip cigarette-ends in a 4.5 L of water for half an hour. This is then strained through a nylon stocking. It will keep several weeks in a stoppered bottle. Diluted in four parts of water it is said to kill even the most hardy of insects. You should not spray it on anything you are going to eat within a fortnight, label the bottle 'Poison', and be sure to wash your hands after using. Obviously this is a strong poison, and you should try the gentler methods first.

One balcony gardener I met stoutly maintains that he is able to keep down aphis by growing the strongly scented marigolds among his plants. This could be worth trying if you don't mind the odour of marigolds. Nasturtiums and chives also have a reputation for repelling certain types of beetles. Chives are invaluable among your plants anyway, and a few bulbs can easily be tucked into the sides of pots holding larger plants.

Constant research is being done in many countries on the question of biological insect control, and it is hoped that the day may come when more and more predator insects will be available to eat up the ones we do not want. I know that already Agricultural Departments in some parts of the United States are able to supply ladybirds, or ladybugs, and the eggs of praying mantids, so it could be worth enquiring from your local State Government Department to see what is available.

However, if you feel that the gentler methods outlined here are insufficient to deal with your pest problem, and that you simply must use an insecticide, do try first those that contain a good proportion of pyrethrum. Make sure it is intended for garden and not household use, of course. Malathion is possibly the next least harmful, but keep in mind that in the close space of a balcony, the harmful fumes will not dissipate as quickly as in the open space of a garden. Also be careful to remember that you will be brushing against the flowers and leaves more often on a balcony, and that pesticides such as malathion should not be in contact with the skin. Also, if you do have culinary herbs growing among your plants, take care that pesticide does not get on their leaves.

The systemic pesticides which are applied to the soil and absorbed by the plants can be very helpful in destroying hard-to-eradicate scale and other pests. Follow instructions on the packet.

Recently the United States Environmental Protection Agency has questioned the use of six pesticide ingredients used in roughly eight hundred separate pesticide products with annual sales of about $US10 million. These are Amoban, Maneb, Nabam, Metriam, Mancozeb and Zineb, which it is stated can break down into a compound called ETU which has been shown in tests on laboratory mice to be a possible cause of cancer and birth defects. Remember to look at the labels on pesticides if you must use them; you can always check with the manufacturer if you are unsure of the contents.

Holiday care

One of the biggest problems facing all gardeners, whether their gardens are large or just little balcony squares, is what to do with the plants during times when they go away. There are several solutions, the best by far of course being the helpful neighbour, or the once-a-week cleaner who can often be induced to do a watering-instead-of-cleaning stint perhaps twice a week, or more if necessary. However, if you are not fortunate enough to possess this kind of co-operation, then it will be necessary to review the most protected areas of your domain, whether indoors or outdoors, into which as many as possible of the plants can be crowded together. I say 'crowded together' advisedly, because they will give one another much more protection and shade in this way and will dry out more slowly than they will standing alone in wind and sun.

If your absence is not to be a long one, put a bucket of water at the centre of a tight grouping of potted plants. Make sure the bucket is standing higher than pots. Have a series of wicks extending from the bucket, one to each pot. Narrow strips of fabric will serve as wicks. Experiment beforehand with what you have on hand to check widths and porosity. Perhaps you

have some thick, absorbent pieces of string? Try it all out beforehand so that you will know just how much water will be transported in this way.

It will not matter if you leave your plant saucers filled with water before you go (unless you'll be away in freezing weather). The plants can then take up this water to tide them over the first few days. A layer of sphagnum moss on the soil surface will do much to retain moisture, as will any flat stones you can add. A piece of clear plastic fitted around the stem and secured to the sides of the pot will create quite a lot of humidity. You can use large plastic bags for this, with the sides cut open. Clear plastic dry-cleaners' bags are very useful here. If you have a number of small plants, this plastic bag technique will serve well if you simply encase the entire pot in the bag and tie the top of the bag around the stem of your plant. Start making a collection of bags in the weeks before you are to go away.

Plastic sheets are very useful too. If your bathroom receives good light you can place all your plants in the bathtub cover them completely with the sheet, taping it to the tub so that the air is almost excluded. They should remain moist for a long period if well watered first. Use quite light-weight sheeting (polythene) of course. It can be bought in varying widths and weights. Should you use this plastic-tent technique, care must be taken that the plants are gradually re-introduced to the outer air. Remember that they will emerge from an unnaturally humid atmosphere, and may even have made new shoots in this 'forcing' temperature. It will be necessary to leave them indoors for a few days, and even for the first day or two to leave them in the plastic bag or tent with the top open to accustom them to normal conditions. Disaster could follow an immediate return to outdoor conditions of sun and wind. You could leave a number of ferns or moisture-loving plants standing in a few cm of water in the bathtub (without plastic covering) if you only plan to be away for a few days, but roots would begin to rot if left for too long.

It is possible to install self-watering systems which automatically water your plants at a certain time each day. Some people use these all the time to avoid daily watering, but there can be problems as all plants do not require the same amount irrespective of weather conditions, but for a few weeks absence they can be very useful, if somewhat expensive. A series of little plastic tubes runs from a series of larger pipes to the soil of each plant, but this too, would need to be well tested out before leaving.

If you can find enough deep planters or containers to hold each pot, these could be packed with sphagnum moss between pot and planter, well watered first. This would hold moisture for quite a time. The surface soil would need a good layer of the moss also. There are other moisture-holding

Brilliant gloxinias will grow quite well on a sheltered balcony if given a few hours of morning sun. They must not be exposed to wind, as both flowers and foliage are brittle and easily damaged.

media such as vermiculite, peatmoss, and chopped plastic foam. Even wet sand could be used, but it dries out more quickly than the moss.

None of these measures however, are as satisfactory as having somebody come in and water, giving them precise instructions about not watering plants which are already moist, or which have water already in their saucers.

Another alternative is to look for firms which specialise in caring for plants, and failing these, try one of those which supply and maintain plants for hotels, apartment buildings, etc. In leaving your plants with such firms, they will at least have expert attention. Even your local nursery might rise to the occasion, especially if you are a client. In the large building where we live, we have a *quid pro quo* arrangement among neighbours in the matter of plant-minding, but those who have to mind *ours* inherit a formidable task!

Index